Praise

'I was expecting this book to t   ......er
than extrinsic motivation, but .. ،ues deeper. I really
like these philosophies, which can be applied equally
to your professional and personal life.'

— **James Montgomery**, VP Engineering,
    Hiber Global

'I really enjoyed this book, which has parallels with
modern psychology and ancient philosophies. The
explanations of honesty, awareness, clarity, courage
and authenticity were useful and practical, and reading
the case studies took me back to the coaching sessions
with Julia.'

— **Miguel Ferreira**, freelance software and
    system engineer

'Julia has a vast knowledge of how the human mind
works, drawn from her many years as coach and trainer.
This is reflected in this inspiring and readable book. It
will not only prompt you to rethink your work environment but spur you into action. Highly recommended
for anyone who works or has ever worked.'

— **Lieke Hallegraeff**, Global Impact Lead,
    FinDock

'This is a useful and readable book for engineers who want to thrive rather than just survive in modern engineering organisations. I learned a lot from Julia's HACCA model and use it every day.'

— **Joep Piscaer**, TLA Lead, TLA Tech

THE
GEEK'S
GUIDE TO
WORK

Be happy and successful in your career

Julia Sullivan

R^e think

First published in Great Britain in 2021 by Rethink Press (www.rethinkpress.com)

Contents

Foreword

If you want to get on in the corporate world you will face many challenges, but the biggest challenge will be the relationship you have with yourself. Your fear of not being the person you think you should be will follow you everywhere, putting pressure on all your relationships, interfering with your sleep and spoiling your weekends. No amount of knowledge or expertise will ever be enough.

The world is changing faster than ever before. Being able to be your true self, and being comfortable with who that is, is no longer a luxury but critical for success. This requires that you work on having a good relationship with yourself (and all those critical voices in your head).

The journey to reaching your goals has ups and downs. Sometimes a step brings you closer to achieving a goal, sometimes it takes you further away from it. How can you maintain the drive to keep going with the same energy and eagerness when things are not going as you had hoped?

I have been working in IT since 1995. First as a developer, then, as I progressed in my career and slowly but surely climbed the corporate ladder, I found myself promoted to senior leadership positions, including VP of a professional services department and now Director IT Architecture of Bol.com.

It hasn't always been an easy ride to get to where I am today. Early in my career I was surrounded by male leaders, who talked and behaved in a certain way. I certainly did not fit that picture. A critical voice in my head would often tell me that I was in no way the right person for this job. It did not matter that I was good at it and people liked working with me. I was my own worst critic. I was worried about what others might think of me, which prevented me from taking the steps necessary to find true happiness in the workplace.

In 2015–2016 I worked with Julia to create a custom leadership programme (based on the HACCA model) for my management team. This training was an eye-opener and had a hugely positive effect on us as a team. We all had different challenges, but what we had in common was that critical inner voice that affected the way we behaved and built relationships with others (including ourselves).

Once we were able to recognise our counterproductive behaviours, we could adjust them. We made these changes stick by practising them over and over. It improved our collaboration with each other, and some of us saw our careers take off as a result and have gone on to great jobs that we love and believe in.

My ability to see and learn from how my own behaviour contributed to an outcome (success or failure) has helped me to grow as a person and reach the position I have today. As well as taming my own inner voice, I can support others to deal with theirs, by knowing how to challenge them to go for their best. As a leader, I know it is important to create a safe environment where people love their work, welcome being challenged, trust their authentic selves, embrace failure and dare to strive for their best.

Building a better relationship with yourself is not something you can achieve through knowledge and insights alone. To make sure it sticks, you need to practise it. This is where Julia's knowledge and experience came into play, training and coaching my team so that their newly learned skills and tools become second nature.

Anyone who wants to can become happier and more successful at work. This book is an excellent starting point for that journey, especially if you want to continue to grow while remaining your authentic self.

Linda Bovaird
Servant leader in tech and
Director IT Architecture, Bol.com

Introduction

This book is for the geeks of the world. If you opened this book, you are probably proud to be a geek. You are someone who knows what it means to take your craft seriously – sometimes a little too seriously, perhaps. You have put in the hours, pulled the occasional all-nighter, and people may have thought you weird at times, but producing great work makes your heart sing. You also know that getting there is not always easy, especially when other people are involved.

I consider myself a geek in my own field. In this book I write not only about what I and my partners talk about in the training room, but how I live my life. I do this not to teach you how to be a geek, but to show you how to be successful and happy in your career. I make no promises that it will turn you into a millionaire – that is up to you – but I can assure you it will help you love being alive.

The human stuff

As soon as you put a group of people together on any complex project, however many standups and retrospectives you hold, processes quickly become complicated by the 'human stuff': the misunderstandings, the disagreements, the disappointments, the overexcitement, the arrogance and the self-doubt. This generates more human stuff, as others in turn react.

Very few tech professionals know how to deal with this part of the job. Many avoid it, believing that the human stuff should be dealt with at home. Others view people skills as something you are either born with or you are not. While thoughts and emotions are often hard to control, few people have learned how to deal with this in practice.

Since I started this work twenty years ago, it has not been uncommon for participants to tell me and my colleagues that it changed their life. For many years I have tried unsuccessfully to explain *why* this work resonates so much. But in the past two decades some exciting new schools of thought in science, economics and history have been challenging the way we look at life, work and reality itself.

Since the onset of the Covid-19 pandemic in 2020, more and more people have been questioning the relationships they have with nature, with themselves, with their loved ones and with work. These exciting new schools of thought go a long way to explaining why this work has such a life-changing effect. With this book I hope to make the link between some of this new thinking, the work my partners and I have been doing and your daily life at work. I hope to show you that thriving at work, especially in the tech field, does not involve working harder. On the contrary. My colleagues and I have supported thousands of professionals to handle the pressure and competitiveness of work while retaining all of their sensitivity, uniqueness, vitality and love for life. I want to show you that you can do it too.

You will learn how to become more effective while staying true to yourself by applying the HACCA model:

- **Honesty:** Hiding your ideas and feedback will hold you and your team back because necessary corrections will not be identified, frustrations will grow and this will affect the extent to which you trust your colleagues and yourself. There is no getting around it – daring to be honest is the start of a new and more exciting relationship with your work.

- **Awareness:** Look around you, use your eyes and ears – what is your environment telling you? Your thinking may be right or wrong, so don't believe it automatically. Once you start looking clearly at what there is you will react more appropriately and effectively and adjust where necessary.

- **Clarity:** A lot of people tend to avoid looking straight at what is and isn't working and rely on their feelings to guide them. Learning to distinguish where facts end and thoughts start will make you clearer-minded, more grounded and realistic. Your confidence and energy in handling things that aren't working will grow, as will your pride in things that are.

- **Courage:** Working with people means encountering other opinions. This will affect your behaviour in many subtle ways – a pacifying comment here, a question not asked there, a defensive reaction here, a moment of self-doubt there. Without noticing it, you will have developed routines of behaviour that are keeping you locked at your current level. Many of these routines relate to how you handle the people around you. Having the courage to identify those habits and change the ones that are working against you will have surprising results.

- **Authenticity:** Just being yourself doesn't make you authentic, as forces like fear, manipulative thoughts and emotions frequently lead you to behave in ways that contradict your intention and that you later regret. Being authentic involves staying true to your intention by mastering your internal environment so that it works for you.

After reading this book, you will see that your industry is less about tech and more about relationships and moral principles. You will be better able to work with your moods and build a more supportive relationship with yourself. You will be confident in your ability to manage your relationships with others. You will know what to do, and when to do it, to keep those relationships healthy.

How to read this book

If you are a manager or a team leader you will know how difficult it can be when your results are dependent on the behaviour of individuals, all with their opinions, prejudices, moods and expectations. If you are managed by someone else, you will be familiar with the pressure that comes with knowing that much hangs on your performance, and will probably have noticed how that knowledge impacts your behaviour.

I wrote this book for people on both sides, to remove some of the mystique around personal development and show what it can do. Personal development is an unprotected profession and, in the past ten years, the number of life coaches has exploded. It is easy to get lost in the plethora of companies claiming to offer transformational programmes for businesses. The result is that many companies waste their training budgets on programmes that create no noticeable shift in attitude or behaviour.

Whether you are a manager or a team member, you are a human being. This book is about how to be great at handling the day-to-day reality of working *as* and *with* human beings.

You can read this book in a variety of different ways, depending on how much impact you want it to have on your life. You can read it like you would any other nonfiction book, in which case you will agree with some parts and disagree with others, relating to the information it presents as an observer. This manner of learning is what I call intellectual learning.

If you want a more interesting and useful journey, one that gets you to discover new things about yourself that are affecting your results, I advise you to take the effort to do the practical assignments at the end of the chapters. In this case, rather than read the book in one go, you should treat it more as a practical handbook, with the chapters and case studies providing context for the assignments. I highly recommend you complete these assignments, because in doing so, you will experience yourself. This is what personal development is about: developing yourself as a person, rather than loading up with information you need to remember. This is where learning becomes experiential, practical and unique to you.

You may find that something that sounds easy in theory is surprisingly tricky in practice, and vice versa. You may find that certain assignments spark resistance, and that others create a sense of relief and power. There is no right and wrong, everyone is different, but the way you respond to each assignment will reveal things about yourself that you may not have been aware of – which is where any good personal development journey starts.

By doing the assignments, you will become less of an observer of the points made within this book and more of a participant. You will start to get a sense of where your relationship with yourself is working (and therefore what to do more of) and where it is not. You will discover where you could increase your effectiveness and happiness by doing something different.

When you have finished reading, fill in the Inspiring Leader Questionnaire at https://Juliasullivan.scoreapp .com, to score yourself against the HACCA model. It will provide you with an analysis of your own particular strengths and weaknesses, and an indication of how you can make your work life easier and more successful.

I wish you an insightful ride.

PART ONE
HONESTY

Speaking your truth, in your way, in your moment

The nature of workplaces is that relationships tend to be interchangeable. You join a project or a company, you figure out who you should be working with, you get to know each other well enough to be able to do your thing, then at a certain point you leave for the next project or company. Some co-workers become true friends; with others you have a more superficial connection. Plus, there is always someone you don't really like – or worse – but you have learned to be professional, so you are civil to everyone and keep a lot of your opinions to yourself. It's an etiquette that keeps workplaces running smoothly, and people who have perfected the art of putting everyone at ease often do well in companies. In many ways, this is a good thing.

After all, who wants to work in an environment where everyone is bickering?

This etiquette has several downsides, however. The first is that when things remain unspoken, they fester. Have you ever noticed what happens when you think someone is unprofessional and push the thought away? It comes back later. After you have pushed it away several times, it gets bigger and starts to bother you, you get frustrated and that hangs in the air. Meanwhile, mistakes continue unchecked.

A second downside to polite professionalism is that relationships stay superficial and, well, interchangeable. You might wonder what's wrong with that. You are used to it and have probably never stopped to think about it. Imagine for a second, though, what it would be like to work with people you trusted with your life and with whom you could express yourself completely. It would be a whole different way of working.

What would it be like to have relationships with your co-workers that are as challenging, joyful and forgiving as those you have with great friends? To work with people you trust and accept and whose unique qualities and limitations you accept, even love. The price of keeping relationships superficial and interchangeable is that they will never become truly great.

ONE
Speak Your Truth

You are not an algorithm. You have a mind. You have thoughts and opinions. You have tendencies, prejudices and sometimes you get emotional. Unlike an algorithm, you have a will of your own – which means you can initiate and be creative. All this and more makes up who you are. If you want to be successful and happy in tech, you must embrace all these aspects of yourself.

Most people think that getting ahead in their career requires working harder and knowing more, hiding the parts of themselves they are ashamed of. This is what we have been led to believe, but it's not true. Those who thrive have one thing in common: they don't pretend to know something when they don't, and they are not trying to prove anything. Dropping your need to prove yourself will revolutionise the way you approach life and work, and turn life into an adventure. Speaking your truth is both critical and a little bit scary at the same time.

The process of running a business of any kind is highly complex. It involves initiating and developing processes, coordinating activities, creating understanding and buy-in between people, developing new processes and products, identifying and correcting mistakes, cataloguing and recording activities and so on and so forth. On a micro level it involves millions of individual decisions and actions. What is critical in all this, is that everyone is speaking up and being honest. I don't mean you should vent all your opinions about everything and everyone – that would create chaos and likely get you fired – but that within the mandate you have, you should speak your mind. Otherwise, frankly, why are you there?

You are part of a whole body of individuals and the way you brief, support, encourage and react to each other are the veins, arteries and nerves of your work. Working well with others is about checks and balances. It is a constant process of trial and error. This finetuning process rests on one fundamental premise: that each person in the team speaks his or her truth.

What does it mean to speak your truth? It means that if something is not clear to you, you ask someone to explain until it is. It means that if you observe something in a process that doesn't work, you speak up about it. If some people always turn up late to team meetings, it means that you say something about it. If the briefing style of one of your colleagues leaves you confused and stressed, it means you tell them.

If you don't say what's on your mind, you and your co-workers will remain stuck in an illusion where everyone is pretending. If I am your colleague and you don't tell me that you don't like the way I interrupt you in team meetings, I cannot correct this behaviour. If I am your manager and my habit of walking past your desk once a day to check on you is making you nervous, if you don't tell me, how can I learn to be a better manager? If I am your co-worker and I don't know what you really think, I will never know for sure where I am with you and I will never feel entirely at ease with you.

Case study: Isabel

Isabel[1] worked for the HR department of a company providing digital products for large brands. She had been referred to me by her manager, who'd told me that she had a lot of potential but could do with some support.

---

1   All names in this book have been changed.

'What brought you here?' I asked her in the intake session.

'I'm very happy with my job,' she said. 'It's just that it is very intense, there is a lot going on and I often feel like I am running after myself. I work long days and have a forty-five-minute train commute. When I get home, it often feels like I haven't achieved anything. I feel chronically tired and exhausted.'

'And what needs to happen for you to say that this coaching has been successful?'

'I want to feel like I'm more in control of my day. That I'm making progress. I also have several colleagues who complain quite a lot and that creates a bit of a negative and tiring atmosphere.'

'What is your role in the company?'

'I am a project assistant in HR and handle all kinds of things, depending on what needs to be done. But I have recently been given a new project, which I'm struggling with. We have a new HR system into which everyone is supposed to input the information about the project they're working on, specifying the hours they have spent on the project and their holiday days. One of my tasks is to get everyone in the company on board and actively using it. It involves quite a bit of internal marketing, helping people find their way around it, and sometimes people notice bugs that need fixing.

It's a lot of work, and some of the project managers are being a little childish about it. They cringe when they see me coming and make jokes, saying that I'm going to tell them off for not using the new system. Then there are others who just send me emails with their information, asking me to input it for them.'

'OK, great. Now give me three or four values that you want to work on during the coaching.'

'More focus would really help me.'

'What do you mean, specifically?'

She raised an eyebrow. I continued, 'My definition of focus is only allowing relevant issues to distract you. Daily, all of us encounter hundreds of distractions. If you apply the value of "focus", this will help you find ways to avoid being distracted from what you want to be working on.'

'OK, I get it. Yes, that would help.'

'You don't want to be too strict though, because some distractions are relevant. For example, if you get a call telling you that you need to go the hospital because your partner has had an accident, you'll want to stop what you are doing.'

'Ah, OK, yes.'

'OK, what other values do you want to add?'

'I want to create more clarity with my co-workers about what we expect from each other.'

'Great. My definition of clarity is distinguishing between objective facts, opinions and feelings. If you feel tired and exhausted, there are probably thoughts and emotions going through your mind that you haven't untangled. I think this could support you.'

'Yes, I think so too.'

'By the way, how often do you acknowledge yourself?'

'Not much,' she laughed, with an expression that suggested she couldn't see how this was relevant.

'Let's add self-acknowledgement to your list. So now we have clarity, self-acknowledgement and focus. Anything else?'

'No. If I manage to apply these, that will be a big help.'

'OK, perfect. Now give me a measurable goal. If you are clear, focused and you acknowledge yourself, what do you hope to achieve in six weeks' time?'

'That I can be leaving work by 5.00pm every day without feeling guilty and that my work still gets done.'

'Perfect. And what will stop you from achieving this? Make a list of everything you can think of.'

She wrote the following list:

- Doing work for others that they should do themselves

- Not saying no

- Thinking, 'Who am I to tell the others what to do?'

- Thinking, 'They are not going to take me seriously'

- Not asking for help

- Not planning, then trying to do everything at once

- Worrying that others will think I'm lazy

I then asked her to take a couple of minutes to write down the specific actions she would need to take to make her six-week goal happen. Her list included the following:

- A conversation with John to clarify what our expectations of each other are, to make it clear that it is up to him to input his own data and to check if he has any questions

- A conversation with Anneke to suggest I have a Q&A with her team about how the system works

- A conversation with my new colleague, Saul, to connect and get to know him better

'OK, perfect. Your homework is to plan those actions into your week and send me an email every forty-eight

THE GEEK'S GUIDE TO WORK

hours to update me on every step of progress you make.'

That week she sent me her update emails and we saw each other a week later. 'Did you make any progress?' I asked her once we had settled down for our second meeting.

'Yes!' She smiled. 'I had the conversation with John, and it went great. I was a bit nervous beforehand because I wasn't sure how he was going to react. John is an informal kind of guy, so I started with a bit of chit-chat and there was a light, jokey atmosphere. I asked what he thought about the new system. He had a bit of a moan about it, so I just let him talk. Then I asked him if I could be honest with him, and he said yes. I told him, in a nice way, that I was struggling with him. That I had tried everything I could to get him to understand how important the system was and that he do his bit, but that it didn't seem to have worked and I didn't know what else to do – and that I was getting tired of having to chase after him.'

'And how did he respond?'

'He was quiet for a moment, then he told me he hadn't realised that he'd upset me, that it hadn't been his intention to make my life difficult. He said that from now on he would input his data himself. Even though he didn't agree with the system, he would do it for me.'

'That's great!' I said. 'There are some specific things that are great about this, and it will help you if we identify them individually.' I listed these for her individually, as follows:

- First, you dared to have the conversation rather than avoid him.

- You thought to adapt the conversation to his informal style.

- He was willing to listen.

- You allowed him to talk, rather than fighting him.

- As a result, he listened to you rather than resisting you.

- You were honest about the fact that you have been struggling with him.

- He heard your feedback.

- He has apologised and resolved to work with the system.

I asked her, 'Do you understand why it helps to break this down into parts?'

'Not really.'

'It helps you to learn from what you did. If any of these parts had been missing, you may not have created the

THE GEEK'S GUIDE TO WORK

result you did. If you focus only on the result, you miss important lessons about how you got that result.'

'That makes sense.'

'OK, now tell me, how is this different from what you were doing until last week?'

'Well, normally, I would be so nervous of his reaction that I wouldn't dare to initiate the conversation. I would swallow my frustration and input the information myself. I would tiptoe around the situation and there would be this elephant in the room.'

'Right. And am I right in thinking that John isn't the only person you do this with?'

'No. I do this with a lot of co-workers. I usually think, "Oh, this isn't such a big deal, what's the point of creating a fuss?" And it isn't a huge deal – it takes me a few minutes to input his data into the system, but it all adds up, so I'm the one who ends up having to stay until 6.00pm and I'm the one feeling tired and frustrated at the end of the day.'

We continued this way through our second meeting, looking at what Isabel had done differently, the results she had created and the insights she had gained.

Your first assignment: Communicating negatives and positives

Imagine for a second that you were able to tap into the minds of all your co-workers and read their unedited thoughts. You would have access to vast amounts of information. Some of that information would be subjective opinions, stories and feelings. But some of that information would be objective and actionable.

Let's say that one of your co-workers came into the office and found that someone had put dirty coffee cups into a dishwasher full of freshly washed plates. Old coffee and dark brown dregs had dripped onto the white crockery below. They consider turning the dishwasher on for another cycle, but decide against it, instead hand washing and drying the dirty cups and plates and putting them in the cupboard. Meanwhile, they may be thinking, 'Which unobservant so and so did this?' and will carry that thought into their day. If this was the third or fourth time this had happened, their mental picture would be that some people in the team were sloppy and selfish. They may decide not to mention it because it isn't that big of a deal, but it would affect the way they feel about their job, the team and the company. The more times it happens, the more their irritation will increase.

This kind of thing is happening all the time. The collective thinking of your co-workers contains huge amounts of valuable information about the practical day-to-day details of how you all go about your daily business: how briefings are conducted, how meetings are run, how lunch is organised, how the temperature in the office is regulated, how food is delivered and so on and so forth. All this is information which, if collected, could inform small daily improvements in the way things are run. Small daily improvements lead to large monthly improvements. In most organisations, thousands of these simple improvements are not identified and so thousands of small frustrations pile up simply because huge amounts of valuable information like this is not communicated.

By contrast, imagine another of your colleagues was sitting at their desk thinking, 'It's so thoughtful that my co-worker brought coffee for me. That rarely happened in my previous job, but I really like that it's commonplace here. It makes me feel at home.' Communicating things like this is easy to do and makes a big difference, but we often keep them to ourselves, simply because we assume they are clear.

ASSIGNMENT ONE

Voice two negative points and two positive points you have been hesitant to speak up about. Communicate them directly to the person concerned – don't talk about anyone behind their back.

TWO

Forget Your Picture
Of Perfection

If you tend to wait and see what others have to say before voicing your opinion, you are not alone. A lot of people are hesitant to speak their mind and the phenomenon of social proof – when people base their opinions and choices on what the majority think – is well-documented in social psychology.[2]

One reason we hesitate before speaking our mind is that we are afraid of being confrontational. A lot of research has been done on conformity and behaviours like banding together, promoting social harmony and

---

2   R Cialdini, *Influence: Science and practice,* 5th edition (Allyn and Bacon, 2008)

not dissenting from the group.[3] Social psychologists and neuroscientists claim we inherited these behaviours from our ancestors, who were under constant threat.[4] Being ostracised or banished could have been a death sentence and a keen awareness of others helped early humans to survive in a dangerous and uncertain world.

You will also have a personal idea of how you think you should behave. If you are someone who hesitates to speak your mind, this probably includes being considerate and not being too loud. You have a picture of perfection in your mind that you measure yourself against. In fact, you don't just have one, you have several. You have a picture of the perfect professional, the perfect manager, the perfect daughter or son, the perfect parent, the perfect lover, the perfect man or woman of your age – you have hundreds of perfect pictures. In your world of perfect pictures, the perfect version of you is better informed and more convincing than the real you. That real you is never quite good enough. The perfect you is always more relaxed, decisive, successful, intelligent or interesting than you, better able to stay calm in a crisis, and so on.

---

3   TJH Morgan and KN Laland, 'The biological bases of conformity', *Frontiers in Neuroscience*, 6 (2012), 87, https://doi.org/10.3389/fnins .2012.00087, accessed September 2021

4   R Boyd and PJ Richerson, *Culture and the Evolutionary Process* (University of Chicago Press, 1985)

You are constantly comparing yourself with picture-perfect versions of all the roles you play, and those perfect versions are constantly reminding you that you are not quite as good as you think you should be. Every time you tell yourself how you 'should be', you are reinforcing this. This is what you do every time you think, 'I should know this,' 'I shouldn't get emotional,' 'I should be faster and more efficient,' 'I should be able to do this presentation in a smooth and relaxed way without sounding nervous,' 'I should be more sociable and show some interest in my colleagues,' 'I should be more successful by now,' or, 'I should have more followers on Instagram'.

The thing is, you believe this internal picture and dialogue to be the truth, that this imaginary image of perfection exists. You look at the gap between that picture and your reality and you see it as proof that you are not 'there' yet. It is little wonder you sometimes feel down and insecure. The problem with these pictures of perfection is that they are continuously changing, like a mirage that you can never reach. You can't win. Sometimes the picture tells you that you should be funnier and more interesting in social situations; sometimes it tells you that you should be richer, or more stylish, more focused, more eco-friendly, more politically engaged. To make things worse, these days social media bombards us with never-ending images of how life 'should' be.

Case study: Naomi

Naomi was thirty years old, worked for a crowdfunding platform and was a participant in the public programme I run, The Essence. Her group had twenty participants, among which she stood out as popular, cheerful, smart and easy-going.

It was day five. The participants and I had been through a lot together in four days full of processes and experiences, and there was a sense in the room (as there always is at this point in the training) that we didn't need to hide anything from each other, that it was safe to say anything. Naomi raised her hand to share, but when I picked her, she stood in front of the group struggling to find the words.

'I don't know how to say this,' she said. 'I am exhausted. It's not about the past few days. I'm exhausted in my life. I am always the cheerful girl, always the positive one. If I have a date with someone and they can't make it, I am understanding and flexible. I tell them, "It's OK, let's reschedule." Whenever there's a problem, I'm the one who offers to help. I am always positive, looking for solutions.'

She explained that since her teens, her easy-going style had won her a reputation as great to work with and she suspected it was one of the reasons she had landed her current job. But she was beginning to tire of it and the pressure to keep up the appearance of cheerful optimism felt like a burden.

'I am exhausted,' she said. 'I feel like I'm putting on a show to keep everyone else happy and that I can't be myself.'

'What are you afraid of? That they might see the person behind the show?' I asked.

'I don't know. That they'll think I'm not that interesting. That I'm selfish. That they won't like me.'

'Is the idea that you're selfish a fact or an opinion?'

'Um...An opinion.'

'Whose opinion?'

'Mine, I suppose.'

'Who says it's true?'

She paused...'Me.'

'Have your friends or colleagues ever told you that you are selfish, or boring?'

She laughed. 'No.'

'But because you never let them see behind the show, you are afraid that it's not you that they love, but your cheerful mask. Is that right?'

'Yes.'

'Tell me, what price have you been paying for hiding behind this pretence?' I asked her.

'That I like myself less and less. That I don't dare to say what I really think.'

'What things have you not been saying?'

'Oh,' she laughed. 'Nothing shocking, little things. Like if I feel disappointed, I don't tell anyone.'

'And what does that do to your self-respect?'

'It goes down.'

'And your sense of pride?'

'That goes down too.'

'Do you want the relationships in your life to be honest?'

'Oh, yes.'

'But you are a liar.' I smiled as I said this, and she looked shocked. I continued, 'You know the words to say, but your actions don't match them. Who is the person who will always know that you're lying?'

'Me.'

'If you are not honest, can you ever have honest relationships?'

'No.'

'If you don't say what you really think, who is it who has been rejecting you all this time, is it your co-workers or yourself?'

'Myself.'

'And has this been painful?'

She nodded, 'Very.'

'Is this what you deserve?'

'No.'

'So, what are you going to do?' I asked her.

'I'm going to start being honest and saying what I think.'

We continued our conversation for a little while and I challenged her to do a few things that she usually would not do out of fear of what other people would think, just a few harmless actions.

'I can't. I don't dare.'

'Well you don't have to,' I said. 'You can take your seat. I love you anyway.'

She remained standing and looked at me. She hated her preoccupation with what others thought and, at that point, she also hated me for challenging her to do something different. She hesitated. Then she went for it. She did a little funny dance. As she did so, a smile crept over her face. She was enjoying it. She transformed into someone playful and fun, more energetic.

At the completion evening four days later, she shared that when she had got back to the office her fears about being perceived as egoistic were quickly put to rest by her colleagues, who complimented her on how clear she had become, how she had a different energy, was calmer and more grounded, and that they appreciated the safety she created for them to be honest.

Your second assignment: Sharing

Psychologist and couples therapist Dr Sue Johnson found that there was a common factor in marriages where one or other person reported feeling lonely or missed the 'chemistry'. It was that conversations had become superficial and mechanical.[5] For whatever reason, one or both partners were keeping their emotional world to themselves and sharing little to nothing of their fears, doubts and inner thoughts with each other. She also found that when both individuals in a couple had the space to express their innermost thoughts without being judged, the relationship vastly improved. Once agreements were made about privacy and allowing each other to have a say, as soon as one of the pair started to share openly, it had an inspiring effect on the other, who then dared to do the same. Marriages that had been distant or tense became warm, caring and loving.

This same principle applies in the workplace, as Google discovered through a study it conducted entitled the Aristotle Project.[6] In 2012, Google launched an in-depth study to find out what differences there were between the teams that struggled to work together and meet their outcomes and those that excelled. They put together a team of statisticians, organisational psychologists, sociologists and engineers, and reviewed studies spanning more than five decades as well as observing every last characteristic of the teams within the organisation.

---

5   S Johnson, *Hold Me Tight: Seven conversations for a lifetime of love* (Little Brown, 2008)

6   C Duhigg, 'What Google learned from its quest to build the perfect team', *New York Times* (28 February 2016), www.nytimes.com/2016 /02/28/magazine/what-google-learned-from-its-quest-to-build-the -perfect-team.html, accessed September 2021

When they set out, they were looking at patterns in how the teams interacted, personality traits of team members, their education levels, hobbies and more, but it soon became clear that individual team member traits were not what gave the more successful teams their edge. When they looked closer at the way the groups worked, there was one characteristic that stood out: psychological safety. Psychological safety is defined as 'an individual's perception of the consequences of taking an interpersonal risk'.[7] In other words, psychological safety is about the extent to which a person trusts that they can be innovative, admit to a mistake or ask a question, without fear of being judged or losing status within the group.

Through Project Aristotle, Google found that the teams that excel are those where team members feel able to contribute equally to any meeting or conversation, trusting that their teammates respect them enough to not reject, embarrass or punish them for doing so. What's more, they found that when the guiding principle is efficiency and co-workers share only what is necessary, relationships become superficial and mechanical. As soon as some team members dare to be vulnerable in sharing thoughts or doubts, others feel safe enough to be honest and speak up about what's

---

7   C Duhigg, 'What Google learned from its quest to build the perfect team', *The New York Times Magazine* (25 February 2016), www.nytimes.com/2016/02/28/magazine/what-google-learned-from-its-quest-to-build-the-perfect-team.html, accessed September 2021

going on with them too, making relationships deeper and more trusting.

ASSIGNMENT TWO

The thing about culture is that it is nothing but the combination of lots of individual actions. How does a culture start to build or change? With one person who dares to do something different.

Your second assignment is to have an open discussion with two people for at least five minutes, in a way or about something that doesn't belong in your picture of perfection. For example, sharing any doubts, thoughts or emotions you would usually keep to yourself.

Choose someone you feel safe with and don't make it a monologue – allow them to share too.

Summary:
Honesty

- Being happy and successful in your work is not about working harder but about speaking your truth and dropping the pretence that you know more than you do, or that you are someone you are not.

- The effectiveness of your team depends on everyone being honest, including you. Being honest means speaking up about both what is and isn't working. That way, you can identify any corrections that need to be made and things that work particularly well can be repeated.

- Fear of being confrontational is one of the reasons you hesitate to speak your mind. The other reason is that you are constantly measuring yourself against a perfect picture of how you could or should be.

- Once one person dares to share their innermost thoughts, including their doubts and fears, they can inspire others to do the same. Teams in which people share like this experience a high level of psychological safety, meaning people feel more at home, more connected, more able to express themselves freely, and they have higher energy and a sense of excitement. It has been proven that teams with a high level of psychological safety are more likely to excel.

- Some people overdo it when giving feedback. Focusing on and criticising others' behaviour is a way of avoiding looking at oneself, and it undermines the psychological safety in a group. Constructive honesty is about looking at your circle of influence and your role within it.

PART TWO
AWARENESS

A state in which we are in contact with our
senses: what we see, hear, smell and touch

We don't realise it, but the way we perceive reality is deeply influenced by a mesh of shared
stories. Any form of human cooperation – whether
as a country, a religion, a tribe or a corporation – is
rooted in common myths that exist only in people's
collective imagination. This ability to construct stories
enabled early human beings to join huge numbers of
individuals who didn't know each other in groups
with a common understanding, similar values and
shared purpose. For thousands of years, myths and
stories have captured the human imagination, pulling
people together, providing meaning and direction.
These myths and stories have made people willing

to leave homes, sacrifice loved ones, give away their possessions, fight and even die for a group or cause.[8]

The reason stories hold so much sway over us is that we often don't see them as 'just stories'. They creep via the back door of our minds into our perception of reality and we see them as the truth. When you pay for your shopping at the supermarket checkout, you don't stop to think that money is an abstract concept rather than an objective reality. Money is a shared story. When you go to work, you probably don't stop to think that the company you work for is also a shared story.

A lot of the narratives we have incorporated into our thinking include attitudes and beliefs inherited over centuries of civilisation. Many of these are outdated, irrelevant or have been proven wrong. For hundreds of years, a lot of our culture's stories have been rooted in science. Since the Enlightenment, we have looked to science to tell us what is true, and scientific proof has become the rubber stamp of reliability. But since the emergence of quantum physics and the mindboggling finding that the behaviour of light as either particles or waves is influenced by the act of being observed, scientists are now admitting that the concept of objectivity itself was a shared story.[9] This was a bombshell. The

8   YN Harari, *Sapiens: A brief history of humankind* (Vintage, 2015)
9   Emerging Technology, 'A quantum experiment suggests there's no such thing as objective reality', *MIT Technology Review* (12 March 2019), www.technologyreview.com/2019/03/12/136684, accessed September 2021

validity of objectivity as the cornerstone of the scientific method is under serious question.[10] Scientists from many different disciplines are now acknowledging that things are far more interconnected than hitherto believed.

What has this got to do with you? You were born into a culture, and you have absorbed the stories of that culture without necessarily noticing them. They have become part of your DNA without you realising it and they affect the way you behave – they determine what you see as real, they inform your concept of normal and they influence what you deem to be possible.

Our stories about humanity are changing

In his book *Humankind*, Rutger Bregman explains that for the last several hundred years there have been two schools of thought regarding fundamental human nature.[11] One school believed that humans require teaching, disciplining, guiding and monitoring to be good, as deep down they are amoral, lazy and selfish. The other school of thought was that, while teaching and guidance may help human beings to grow, they are inherently good. To cut a long story short, the first school of thought won.

---

10 R Healey, 'Quantum Theory and the Limits of Objectivity', *Foundations of Physics*, 48/11 (2018), pp1568–1589

11 R Bregman, *Humankind: A hopeful history* (Bloomsbury, 2019)

This theory has both positive and negative elements. The positive is that our ability to stand up for number one helped us to win the evolutionary struggle for survival, by making us creative, intelligent, resilient and strong, giving us a competitive edge over earlier human species. The negative is that it suggests we are not natural collaborators, that we need to be taught to curb our desires and be kind to others. If you look at traditional education systems, religions and organisations, they are based on a common premise: that people need to be taught, corrected, motivated and managed to become decent human beings.

This narrative became known as the varnish theory, and the implication is that under the civilised surface (or varnish) of any individual is a selfish, lazy and amoral core of base desires. For many years, this narrative has informed Western institutions – our education systems, our prison systems, our tax systems and our bureaucracies. Lots of management schools are still designed around the idea that motivating, teaching, checking and correcting people is the way to get the best out of them. But, Bregman reveals, more recent science has suggested that the varnish theory is wrong and that the experiments designed to prove it were based on faulty methodology. Palaeontologists now believe it wasn't superior strength or intelligence that allowed us to survive over the other early human ape species, it was our ability to read and react to subtle emotions, to create strong friendships, to learn from and inspire each other. The 'survival of the fittest' theory has been replaced with the 'survival of the friendliest'.[12]

What's so important about this? Well, the narrative that humans are inherently bad, lazy and amoral (and that if you leave them to their own devices things will go wrong) has found its way into the fabric of the culture you grew up in and you are carrying traces of it in the way you think. Every time you criticise yourself for making a mistake, it's there. Every time you get angry with yourself for not trying harder, it's there. Every time you feel shame, it's there. Every time you wonder whether you are good enough, it's there. And without a doubt this is affecting both your happiness and your effectiveness in your work.

Even though this and other related narratives have been found to be untrue, they still influence your thinking and behaviour. We all keep these beliefs alive in the way we communicate with ourselves, our partners, children and the people we work with. And, because we haven't stopped to question these beliefs, we have no trouble finding evidence to support them.

For many years, the story that humans are inherently lazy and selfish and need motivating and monitoring was taken to be the truth and those who claimed

---

12   B Hare and V Woods, *Survival of the Friendliest: Understanding our origins and rediscovering our common humanity* (Random House, 2020)

otherwise were dismissed as naïve hippies. Similarly, for many years we looked at the world based on a story of separation. We learned that a tree is separate from a bird, is separate from an insect – and anyone who claimed that a tree could communicate with a bird would have prompted some raised eyebrows. But scientists are now discovering that trees communicate with each other via microscopic fungal networks in the ground,[13] and that they release hormones into the air that influence the movements of insects and birds.[14] We are discovering that things are far more interconnected than we previously thought, and that many of the stories and the science (which itself is a story) we used to interpret reality were wrong.

A question arises: if we can't rely on the concepts we have been taught, how do we know what is right? The answer is to learn to approach your own thinking with a healthy scepticism, to start putting some distance between you and the many stories you have inherited and never questioned. Training your thinking to work for you is about questioning the stories you have internalised without realising it and recognising that they are just that – stories. The first step in this process is to develop your alertness to what is real and what is a story.

---

13   P Wohlleben, *The Hidden Life of Trees* (Harper Collins, 2017)
14   G Ferguson, *Eight Master Lessons of Nature* (Penguin, 2019)

THREE

Let Go Of Your Need To Be Right

The prospect of being honest with your co-workers may make you feel a bit uncomfortable. There is something threatening about being truly honest. Why is that? Let's take a look.

You, like lots of people, have probably developed your own way of getting along with people and overcoming the minor confrontations that daily life brings. Some people laugh a lot, others have developed a particular sense of humour; some have adopted a style of being interested, or even concerned, others of talking about sport; some people stay entirely aloof. Whatever it is, you have probably found a manner of interaction that you feel comfortable with and the idea of agreeing to be truly honest with your co-workers may feel like a threat to that comfortable status quo.

In a previous life, I worked for a subsidiary brand of Levi Strauss. The company ran an annual HR programme which involved asking three colleagues for honest feedback. Everyone used to get nervous about it when it came round each year; a buzz of fear would hang in the air until the feedback task was over. The first time a colleague asked me for feedback I had just completed a personal development programme and believed passionately that honest feedback could support someone in their growth, so I was eager to put this into practice. Full of enthusiasm and good intentions, I gave her my straight and honest feedback like a bull in a china shop. To make matters worse, I sent it to her by mail. She was deeply hurt by what I said and didn't speak to me for almost a year. You see, a lot of people are extremely sensitive to correction. When we get a piece of negative feedback from someone, most of us are quick to see it as an attack and so we behave defensively. Why?

We are all protective of our picture of reality and the blend of ideas and stories it is based on, because it is familiar and we have learned to work within it. We feel comfortable and at home in that reality. We want our ideas and stories to be right. We don't want to hear where they may be wrong. Agreeing to be honest with each other means welcoming other pictures of reality, and that means exposing ourselves to the possibility that our pictures may be wrong.

You will have based a lot of your past decisions on the stories you believe, so it's little wonder you might be reluctant to let go of them. Admitting that our pictures and stories are wrong feels like admitting we ourselves are or have been wrong. It feels uncomfortable, and it hurts. In response, we revert to one of our favourite habits, a desire to be right. We love to be right because we have learned that being right means we are smart, trustworthy, valuable, successful and so on. We strive to be right and at school we learned how to prove we are right through logical reasoning. We explain our points of view and use the word 'because' to show the logic behind our decisions and arguments. When things are going badly and we want to prove that this isn't our fault, we are quick to defend ourselves with excuses and stories that sound logical. They don't do much to help the situation, but we like to think they help us save face. We can be extremely creative in explaining, defending and proving that our thoughts are right, even when we pay a heavy price for this.

Learn to take your thoughts and opinions less seriously, stop justifying and defending yourself and you will discover that new possibilities open up when you dare to admit you were wrong.

Case study: Ravi

Ravi was an engineer who had been hired by a scale-up that saw his expertise and scientific training as a valuable addition to their management team. His manager had put him in contact with me following a bumpy first three months. The plan had been for him to join the team as a 'free agent' to get acquainted with the company and identify their challenges and areas of development before crystallising his role officially. Since his arrival, though, there had been consternation and upset in the department he had been assigned to.

We met over Zoom in the first month of the Covid-19 lockdown in the UK, and I saw a gentle and sensitive fast-thinker. When I asked him what his purpose was with coaching, he said he wanted to learn to communicate better. He described how, since he had joined the company, he'd been trying to get to know the project managers to observe their processes and help them improve, but that the atmosphere had quickly turned sour. There was now so much tension and hostility that it was not only preventing him from doing his job, but making him deeply unhappy.

'I don't know what's going on,' he said with a sense of powerlessness. 'I don't understand it. All I want to do is to help, but I can't get any of them to listen to me. Whatever I say seems to make matters worse.'

When I asked him what he wanted to get out of the coaching, he told me he wanted to improve the atmosphere with his colleagues. At one point in that first meeting, I asked him, 'What kind of relationships do you want, honest or fake?'

'Oh, honest,' he said.

'Do you realise that honest relationships don't come cheap?' He looked at me quizzically. 'If you want honest relationships, you will have to pay a price. The price is a willingness to hear what others have to say. Are you willing to pay that price?' He laughed. 'You see,' I continued, 'It's easy to say you want honest relationships, but the test is whether you mean that in practice.'

I gave him a tool, a five-step process to use whenever he sensed that he had annoyed someone. The five steps were as follows:

1. Invite the person to be honest. Let them talk freely. Don't interrupt them.
2. Ask them to tell you what exactly happened, from a practical perspective. The cause of upset is always something that happened that should not have, or something that did not happen that should have. Make sure you get to the specifics.
3. Ask the person what they suggest as a solution.
4. Consider their suggestions.
5. Clarify what you are going to do with their suggestions, including any actions that you will not be carrying out and any points that you need to check.

His homework was to have at least two conversations like this with co-workers.

The following week, I asked him how things had gone. He told me he'd had a conversation with the woman he had the most tension with; she had got emotional, and he said it was difficult.

'She was tense. There was a lot of built-up frustration.'

'How did you react?' I asked.

'She accused me of being arrogant and wanting to take over. I tried to explain to her that I was trying to help, but she wouldn't listen.'

'So she pressed your buttons, and you forgot your intention to allow her to talk freely,' I teased.

He tried to object, noticed what he was doing and thought better of it. 'Yes, actually you are right,' he laughed.

'Next time you speak to her, when your defences go up and you feel the need to defend yourself, count to ten and let her talk. Don't tell her to keep calm. Don't object. Just listen. If there is an emotional outburst, allow her to let off steam. Then, find it in yourself to want to hear the facts from her perspective. Ask her – in a calm voice – to tell or show you what you did that you shouldn't have done, or what you didn't do that you should have done. The what, when and where should be so clear that you remember the exact occasion she's talking about. If you don't, ask her for examples.'

The next week, he had done it. I asked him to tell me how it went.

'It was so difficult to keep my mouth shut and not defend myself, but I did it. I bit my tongue and let her speak, and I asked her to give me examples of what she meant. I have done this in the past, but my underlying attitude was always of wanting to prove the other person wrong,' he explained. 'This time, when I asked for examples, it was to learn. That felt different. It created a completely different vibe. She settled into the conversation and we really listened to each other. She made some valuable points that I hadn't thought of before.'

'What did you learn from the conversation?'

'I learned that from her perspective, having someone like me come into the department was difficult. I learned that the way I have been asking questions in meetings sounds like I am attacking people.'

'And what are you going to do with this information?'

'I am going to listen much more.'

Your third assignment: Inviting different perspectives

When you live in your thoughts (as most of us do), it's easy to build castles in the air. Your mind is constructing an imaginary reality on a daily basis. The mind creates meaning by constructing mental models for events you see happening around you, cross-referencing them against what you already know and connecting it all up to create meaning.[15] Because these meanings make sense to you, you allow them to take up residence in your mind, you get used to them and, very quickly, these models of reality feel like home.

As you can imagine, this is a process that can quickly lead you down a lonely rabbit hole. If you were a healthy peasant farmer living in the fifteenth century, your daily life would have been completely rooted in physical reality. Getting lost down mental rabbit holes is not something you would have had to worry about. If you wanted to check whether your farming techniques were working, you would walk down to the pig pen and have a good look at your pigs. You would see how heavy they looked, watch how they moved, how they squealed and interacted with each other and responded to you. Then you would wander through your fields, pinch your crops, smell the ground and listen to the

---

15 T Wujec, 'Three ways the brain creates meaning' (TED Talks, 2009), www.ted.com/talks/tom_wujec_3_ways_the_brain_creates _meaning/transcript?language=en, accessed September 2021

wind. You would observe how things are growing and that would tell you everything you needed to know about whether your methods were working or you needed to change something.

By contrast, people in the twenty-first century spend a great deal of their life in their thoughts. You need to find a way of gathering input from the environment outside your own mental bubble. Look for people who have a different perspective and see things that you don't; people who can show you aspects of your projects that you haven't thought about. Although it feels more comfortable spending time with people who share your views, this will make you lazy and complacent and your mental blindspots will only grow bigger.

Making a habit of looking for and inviting input from people with a different perspective will not only improve your decision-making, but also develop your wisdom as a human being. The more you do it, the more you will discover that being right is vastly overrated and that being wise is a whole different kettle of fish. As you learn to free yourself from your ego, little by little you will realise that not knowing something doesn't make you worthless and that it's OK to be wrong.

ASSIGNMENT THREE

Your third assignment is to identify three co-workers who will be able to offer you a different perspective on something and challenge your thinking. Arrange to have a conversation with them so you can learn from their different experience and knowledge.

FOUR

Look Carefully At The Whole Picture

A lot of people are so caught up in work and domestic chores that they don't stop to look at where they are. Heads down, brains bent around whatever projects they are working on, they are so busy striving to achieve some future goal or state that they don't stop to take a rain-check on where they are in their lives.

Just like the farmer leaning on a fence on a hill surveying their land, it is a good idea to every now and then stand up, put the projects you are working on to one side, look at where you are in your life and ask yourself if you like what you see.

When doing this, you should bear in mind a couple of simple truths. The first is that tangible facts and your opinions of them are two totally different things. Most of us are so used to inhabiting the thinking part of our minds that we forget that our opinions are not facts. A lot of people say they love their life or they hate their life. Others find life boring. Some are ambivalent. These are all opinions.

A tangible fact could be that you have a garden of 20 square metres. Whether you think it's big or small, beautiful or ugly is a matter of opinion. Another tangible fact could be that your job that pays you 3,000 euros per month. Whether you think that is a lot or not enough is again a matter of opinion.

You don't want to assess your life based on opinions; you want to look at it as dispassionately as possible. Your perception is, and will always be, subjective, but you can increase your objectivity by training yourself to identify where you are treating your opinions as indisputable facts and where your thinking is wrong. You want to take a calm detached look at all areas of your life – all the different projects you are involved in at work and at home – and simply ask yourself, 'Is this working?'

The second truth to bear in mind is that everything in life has a benefit and a price. A bar of chocolate has a price of a few euros and the benefit is that it tastes good.

Your house has both a price (the cost of the mortgage and maintenance) and various benefits (it provides you with a stable and comfortable place to rest, cook, eat and receive guests).

Everything we have in life, and everything we do, has a price and a benefit (or benefits). Just ponder this for a second – you can accept this reality without feeling at all uncomfortable. Everything about you has prices and benefits too. It's not good, it's not bad, it's just the way it is. Working eighty hours a week may get you the corner office, but if you were planning to have a great relationship and some children too, you should consider what the consequences are for your private life and if you are OK with them. In the future that price may become too high to tolerate. Some people enjoy smoking, but it comes at a price. You can ignore the health risk and be heartbroken and angry if you get cancer. Or you can see the risk of cancer as a price you are willing to pay for the pleasure.

There will be parts of your life that work for you and parts that don't. This doesn't mean that you are a bad person or you aren't successful. The question is, do you want to choose how you live your life, or do you want to merely survive, because that's just the way it is? The act of standing back, looking at the whole picture of your life and assessing what's working for you and what isn't, will allow you to make a choice.

Case study: Christina

At the start of 2019, Christina phoned me for help. She was running a team of young, bright, willing developers at a company making payment systems. Christina was getting snowed under by queries, checks and questions from her team and wanted to find a way of getting them to stand on their own feet. She acknowledged there were ambiguities and challenges but was confident that this intelligent young group were up to handling them. The issue was how to get them to take ownership.

Through our conversation, we identified that the past year had brought about a significant change for everyone. The company was the brainchild of two pioneers who had set it up two years previously and the team of developers they had put together had got used to working day and night, living on coffee and take-away pizzas delivered to the office. The startup phase had been crazy but exciting. Everyone was on the same wavelength and, as they pulled in more and more people, the team grew from six to twenty-eight in two years. In the spring of 2019, the startup had been bought by a large American fintech company.

'It is clear that everyone wants to make this work, but there is a sense in the team that you have to be positive. It's like everyone is putting on a brave face. People are working really hard, so sometimes tempers get short and criticism is seen as negative,' Christina told me.

We decided to start with a team session in which everyone was invited to have their say. We made it clear we didn't want them to put a positive spin on things; we wanted them to speak their truth. We divided the team into groups of people who didn't know each other well, and they were asked to prepare an honest list of issues they thought needed addressing. In a second breakout session they were asked to prepare a list of practical solutions to solve those problems. We also stipulated that they had to ensure every member of the group had equal airtime, to ensure the louder ones didn't take over.

You could sense that people were a little wary at the start, but they soon got that we'd really meant it when we'd asked them to be honest. Nothing that they said would be used against them, the only requirement was that the feedback should be factual and actionable. The group quickly started to relax and open up, and by the end of the morning they were talking energetically – what is more, everyone was involved, not only the dominant team members.

The first thing that struck Christina was that team members were speaking up about points she had never heard raised before and, on the whole, these points were practical and relevant. Twenty flip-over sheets of issues and solutions were collected, many of which could be implemented immediately, for example, 'The coffee machine needs cleaning,' 'The reception area looks messy,' 'There is a lack of clarity on who the client contact is on project X.' Some were more interpersonal observation, such as, 'We rarely give each other compliments,' 'We aren't proud enough of what we have done,' and, 'I sometimes bust my gut to finish a project on time, then the project is shelved and no one tells me.' For every issue raised there was a suggestion as to how to solve it and an owner was assigned. Meanwhile, the fact that certain behaviours were highlighted as undesirable created insights and opportunities for self-reflection.

In the next breakout session, the groups made a list of things that were working well. These included, 'the flexibility to come and leave when I want', 'the trust that I can figure things out myself', 'that X orders pizza for us in the evening', and 'the location of the office'.

The exercise was quite an eye-opener for Christina and the other directors. Some of the items on the 'what works' list were things they had never thought about, and many of the 'what doesn't work' points were issues that could be easily resolved. They were happy that it was now clear what was going on and how the team wanted to address the issues they had.

Over the course of this exercise, Christina also sensed something else that had nothing to do with action points. She noticed that something had changed in the atmosphere. There was a sense of relief in the team that all these relatively small things that had been building up and irritating them for months were going to be solved that afternoon. They had been allowed to stop pretending and tell the real story.

Your fourth assignment: Observing what is

There is rarely a moment in the day when you are not thinking. Thinking about events from the past and about plans for the future that may or may not happen, and of course about the thoughts and opinions you have about these. In doing so, you build an inner mental reality of rooms, tunnels and landscapes that light up and cloud over with every new thought association, doubt or insight.

The upside of this is that it means you are creative. You can use your thinking to design constructions, products and plans that have never existed before. But this creativity comes with a serious downside: you have become so adept at building inner mental realities that you became a victim of your own deception and react to your pictures as if they were the only realities. Your moods change as you follow your thinking, and in turn your thinking is influenced by your moods.

A lot of people tend to build their inner reality through stories. We humans like to analyse, understand and explain the things in our life – why certain things happened and others didn't, why some things went wrong and others went right, why someone behaved in a particular way. We like to identify the causes and the consequences of a problem. As though we're watching them play out at the cinema, these stories get our emotions going and generate whole landscapes of feelings.

Stories about things we are proud of make us feel powerful, strong and great; stories about disappointments, bad luck and unfairness make us feel indignant, angry and powerless.

The thing is, in the stories we base our mental reality on, the scriptwriter, narrator and director (and often the main character) are the same person: us. This means there is no one checking the story for accuracy. All those emotions feed back into the story and colour the facts, the sequence and the tone of the narrative. A little exaggeration here, an omission there, some vagueness there, all dished up with a thick wallop of emotion and the ego has crafted a story it can chew on for days, weeks, years, even decades. All the while, the ego believes that story to be true.

The simplest way of preventing your stories from taking hold and ensuring you stay in contact with reality is by developing acute physical senses. Never let your thoughts, ideas and plans become more important than what your physical environment is telling you. Don't forget, we are mammals. We can smell, hear, see, and feel the wind on our skin. Develop your senses. When you walk into a room, there is a vast amount of information you can collect simply by looking at people's body language, by noticing sounds, physical sensations in your body, even smells. This sensory alertness is what awareness is about. Most people are so busy transmitting that they forget to observe. To develop your awareness, you may need to speak less and listen more.

ASSIGNMENT FOUR

Your fourth assignment is to do the following:

Make two lists, one of what isn't working and one of what is working in your life. No stories. Make your points factual and quantifiable. Go into detail and look carefully at the following areas:

- work
- family
- love and sex
- parenthood
- finance
- health and fitness
- relationship with self

Ask yourself what is happening that should not be, or what is not happening that should be.

Have two conversations with people in which you consciously focus on listening and watching. Don't act weird, simply make a note to yourself to turn your sensory antennae on during the conversation.

Summary: Awareness

- We have inherited various stories and concepts from our culture, and these influence the way we think about what is possible and what is real. Many of our past decisions were based on these concepts and stories, so we are often reluctant to admit they were wrong. If we are not careful, we can get more tied up in trying to prove we are right than in trying to get things working.

- There is always an identifiable source of disappointment – something that should have happened but didn't, or something that happened that shouldn't have. If you perceive some else's honesty as a personal attack, this is a sign that you believe a negative story about yourself.

- Making a habit of asking for input from people with different points of view will keep you alert and prevent you from getting too attached to your thoughts. If someone in your team is negative towards you, it is likely they are carrying a disappointment. Inviting them to share their disappointment, identifying the facts of the situation and welcoming it as an opportunity to learn will alleviate the negative atmosphere. It will restore trust and provide you with useful information.

- Looking dispassionately at your life and seeing what is and isn't working helps keep you alert. It shows you where you can learn and stops you from taking your life for granted.

- Sharpening your physical senses – your sight, hearing, sense of touch, taste and smell – will keep you aware of your surroundings and prevent you from getting lost in your stories. It will make clear which problems exist in the external world and which exist only in your inner world.

PART THREE
CLARITY

When we separate physical facts
from thoughts and feelings

The extent to which we enjoy our life is determined by an ongoing loop in our thinking that compares our actual experiences to our expectations. It then forms an opinion and generates a feeling – which is another experience. If we expect raising a family to be a series of beautiful, proud moments, we accuse ourselves of being bad parents the moment we feel stressed and cross. If we play tennis and expect to strike each ball with confidence and grace, then every time the ball hits the net we are disappointed with ourselves. This loop controls us and our quality of life. Escaping it entirely is impossible, but learning to distinguish between physical reality, thoughts and feelings will loosen the loop's hold and give you more control over your feelings.

Alongside the conversations we have with the people around us, we are all in an ongoing conversation with ourselves. And when I say ongoing, I mean all day long. It is a constant commentary running through our minds as we go about our day. This internal conversation determines how we feel and react.

It works a little bit like this: you take a sip of your coffee. Your mind watches this happening and thinks, 'Hmm, this coffee tastes nice.' You take another sip.

At work, it might go more like this: you notice your colleague is grumpy and low in energy. 'Hmm, I feel uncomfortable,' you think to yourself. 'Is he angry with me? Shall I leave my question and come back later, or shall I ask?' You decide to ask. Your colleague cuts you off mid-question. 'Damn, I knew I shouldn't have asked.' You excuse yourself and leave the room. 'Now I feel really bad. That was stupid of me. Why was I so clumsy?'

This loop of internal dialogue is going on incessantly and at lightning speed. Occurrence, thought, feeling, reaction (which itself is another occurrence), thought, feeling, reaction/occurrence, thought, feeling, reaction/occurrence, thought, feeling...and so on and so forth. You probably won't be surprised to learn that when our thoughts resist the occurrence (ie when we dislike what we see/hear happening) we feel bad, and when our thoughts accept the occurrence, we feel good.

As we go through our day, this internal mental dance is ongoing, as our thoughts create feelings that trigger reactions that influence our thoughts. Sometimes this merry-go-round of thoughts and feelings gets us feeling good about ourselves and wanting to act, and sometimes it leaves us feeling grumpy, down and tired.

The problem is that all we notice of this activity is the output. We note that we are feeling good and ready for action, but we don't realise that we got there via a sequence of thoughts, feelings and reactions. Or we admit we are feeling grumpy, down and tired, but we are not aware of the thinking process that brought us to that point.

Clarity is about distinguishing between thoughts, feelings and facts. This process of untangling will support you to see through the workings of your mind and notice where it got the better of you. Developing a practice of not automatically believing your thinking will help you develop a sceptical but kind relationship with your mind, like the relationship a parent has with their young child – aware that at any moment they could do something silly and you may need to intervene.

FIVE

Face Up To What Is Not Working

It sounds counterintuitive, but facing up to the specifics of what is not working in your life and being honest about which particular aspects you are not happy with, is one of the most constructive things you can do for yourself. The happiest and most fulfilled people I know are those who are the most honest with themselves and dare to look directly at the truth in their lives.

Most people are very bad at specifying honestly and clearly what is and isn't working in their life but continue to complain that things are difficult and not getting any better. For example, you don't feel great about your weight: exactly how many kilos overweight are you? Is it really your weight that is bothering you, or your lack of vitality and the fact that you feel sluggish? Identifying the nature and extent of any problem is the first step toward solving it. You feel stressed about your finances: how much money do you need to cover your living costs each month, and what exactly is your shortfall? If you think your love life isn't great, what exactly is missing? Is it that you have a partner but you don't talk anymore? Or that you are single and want a partner? Or maybe you have a partner and the two of you talk a lot, but you don't have sex much anymore. The consequence (your dissatisfaction) is the same, but the cause is very different. If you don't identify exactly what the problem is, you can't solve it. You have negative feelings about your work. What exactly are those feelings? Is it stress and the fear of not being able to deliver? Are you disappointed about something that happened? Is there a disagreement or an unresolved conflict with someone? Is it that your role isn't clear? Or is it that you can't stop criticising yourself?

It's not rocket science. To fix a problem, the first step is to know what the problem is, but people are often reluctant to be honest about negative things in their life. They are worried that others will see them as unsuccessful, that they will sound like an attention seeker, or that it will send them into a spiral of negativity. Most people have become experts at not noticing what is not working in their life. They avoid thinking about it. The problem with that is that, if you don't clearly see what is not working, you can't see what *is* working. A lot of people are bored by their work, have no sense of partnership with their colleagues, live with chronic stress and get through life just waiting for their next holiday. If they were to make a list of what isn't working in their life, they likely wouldn't mention any of these things. Our minds are extremely good at avoiding thinking about things. So good, in fact, that we can be blind to what is and isn't working and totally unaware of what's happening. Failing to notice the truth is the same as avoiding the truth. Your mind, like most people's, is well-practised at this.

Without your realising it, your mind has developed a whole variety of escape mechanisms. If you listen carefully, you can pick these out in the language that people use. For example generalising, keeping things vague and talking in sweeping statements is an escape because it allows us not to be specific. A lot of the words and phrases we pepper our speech with are ways of keeping things vague: 'you could say that', 'in some ways', 'kind of', 'on the one hand... but on the other hand'. These are all ways of not pinning our thoughts down, allowing us to sit on the fence and keep things foggy. The most common is 'yes... but', which is the perfect way of making it look like we agree with something, while sneaking our disagreement in through the back door.

Another common way of avoiding what is not working in your life is focusing on other people – the government, the media, the national football team, your manager, your partner, or anyone else you may have

THE GEEK'S GUIDE TO WORK

an opinion about. Many see it as a sign of character to have strong opinions and a lot of people spend more time broadcasting their opinions about others than examining themselves. Since the arrival of social media, this trend has exploded.

The problem with all these escape mechanisms is that they keep things foggy and prevent us from getting to the real issue. Avoiding the issue is tempting because we don't really want to go there. But if you can't get to the bottom of an issue, you can't solve it and so you are left with a sense of dissatisfaction that you don't like and are a bit ashamed of. You cover it up and pretend you are OK. You try harder to be positive, professional and smart, because you don't want to be seen as a loser or a complainer. This doesn't make the sense of dissatisfaction go away, it makes it worse. Meanwhile your anxiety increases because you know you are hiding who you really are. You worry that deep down you aren't the smart, professional person you are pretending to be. Because you are hiding your true self, your doubts about who you are grow. You trust yourself less and less; you like yourself less and less.

Everyone carries self-doubt. The so-called 'imposter syndrome' is a perfectly normal tendency every person has, which is to doubt whether they are good enough. The problem lies in the approach lots of people adopt to deal with this, which is to try and prove that they are smart. Because they have internalised the story perpetuated by our culture that intelligence is about knowing a lot, making few mistakes and being able to argue and speak convincingly, this is what they try to do. The problem with this story is that:

- You equate making mistakes with failing, so you become cautious and criticise yourself for any mistakes you make.

- You become a terrible listener – you are quick to defend and anxious to have the last word (to show you know what you are talking about).

- You find it more important to show you are right than to admit you were wrong, learn and correct.

Case study: Patrick

Patrick was a team leader for a payment technology company. He was in his early thirties and had previously worked for a bank in the city in London. 'I'm not really sure why I'm here,' he said at the beginning of the training. 'I always do my best to learn new things and I'm sure I can learn something from this programme, but I'm not yet sure what. I'm doing well in my career; I have a great job. I have a good relationship, a very nice lifestyle. I consider myself extremely privileged. I don't really have any issues.'

'Well, I'm certainly not going to persuade you into thinking you have issues,' I replied. 'You said you like learning. What in particular would you like to learn in this programme?'

He thought for a second. 'I feel I'm working quite hard with my team.'

'Can you expand?'

'Well, it always feels like I'm the one driving things forward. I don't feel they own it, and I don't know how to get them to sharpen up and be more on the ball. I have this sense that if I don't run after people and check on them, things won't happen. I don't understand how they can be so lacking in initiative. I've tried to get them to take more ownership, but it hasn't worked yet.'

He gave an example of a technical bug that someone in his team had noticed but that had been 'forgotten' and hadn't been corrected a month later. 'I just don't get how they make mistakes as big as that.'

'What prices do you pay for this?' I asked him. 'By prices, I mean what are the negative consequences? These can be practical, like the amount of time spent in meetings, missed earnings, lost clients. Or they could be long hours and not getting home before 9.00pm, interrupted sleep, tension with your partner, tiredness and negative feelings.'

'It exhausts and infuriates me,' he replied quickly.

'What form does your exhaustion take? How do you experience it?'

'I am used to working on coffee, adrenaline and pressure. When I was working for the bank in London there were nights when I would stay in the office until 2.00am, take the underground home to have a shower and change my clothes, and then be back in at 8.00am the next morning. I am good at covering up my tiredness.'

'Does that affect your patience?'

'Oh, definitely. I can get angry. A couple of times I completely lost my temper with someone in my team. In the city, I was on the receiving end of a manager's temper myself a couple of times. It was kind of scary, but it gave me a thick skin. I learned to set the bar high and not to accept less than the best.'

'How does your anger impact your mood when you go home and spend time with your girlfriend in the evening?'

'I get home brittle and irritated. I let off steam to her for a few hours over a couple of beers. It's usually quite a monologue.'

'How is that for her?'

'She has told me a few times that she doesn't like it. It creates a heavy, unpleasant atmosphere.'

'And how does your anger affect the team? Do they pay a price for it?'

'Yes, they do, I'm afraid. A month ago I got so angry with one of my team members that he broke down in front of me. He avoided me for two weeks and he has now left the company. I guess it's not great for their self-confidence.'

'If it's not great, what is it?'

'It undermines their self-confidence,' he admitted.

'Do you see that saying, "It's not great for their self-confidence," rather than, "It undermines their self-confidence," is a way of avoiding?' I asked. 'The escape mechanism is just one of the ways your mind skirts round the truth. Your mind is slippery, it doesn't want to go there, so it evades the truth. What is the benefit in that?'

'That I can continue doing what I have been doing, I don't need to correct myself.'

We let the subject rest for the remainder of day one. The next afternoon, Patrick, like all the other participants in the training, set to work on a self-awareness process. It involved him being truthful about what wasn't working and about his unconstructive behaviour, which had either created unwanted results, made issues worse, or allowed them to remain unresolved. He found himself a quiet corner in the hotel lobby and began filling in the task sheet. The first step was to make a list of every single result in his life that was not working for him at that point in time. When I walked past and glanced at his sheet, he had written 'My anger, the passivity in my team'.

I corrected him, 'Your anger is not a result; it's your behaviour. What are the consequences of your anger? That is what I mean by unwanted results. For example, is there a negative atmosphere at home sometimes?'

'Yes, but not always,' he objected. 'Things are usually pretty good.'

'Nice escape mechanism!' I smiled. 'How often do you come home irritated? Is it closer to once a year or once a fortnight?'

'Once a week.'

'And what else is not working in your life? Anything at all, write it down.'

After our conversation, his list looked like this:

- Our living room is full of unpacked removal boxes.

- There is a negative atmosphere at home on average once a week.

- Ongoing discussion with my partner about a holiday this year hasn't been resolved.

- I rarely get home before 7.00pm.

- I haven't been to the gym for two months.

- We haven't had a romantic evening together for over a year.

- I haven't spoken to my brother for six weeks.

- There is lack of clarity around the issues slowing Project A.

- Project B is running a month behind schedule.

- Client X is unhappy and threatening to take steps.

- Team Member B is on sick leave.

- Status on Work Group C is unclear.

- No one in my team speaks their mind.

I left him to continue the list in his own time. An hour or so later everyone was done with the process, we were back in the training room, and he raised his hand to share.

'What I had never realised before is that my behaviour is driven by a belief I didn't know I had, which is that I have to be in control.'

'How does that manifest in how you interact with others?' I asked.

'Things have to be done the right way – which is my way, in my time frame.'

'OK. And what if they aren't? Imagine a hypothetical situation where things get completely out of hand, and don't go at all the way you had envisaged. What would you think about yourself?'

'Oh, I would hate that. It would make me feel weak and unprofessional.'

'And what would be the worst thing that someone could possibly think about you?' I asked.

'That I am weak,' he admitted.

'What do you do to make sure that doesn't happen?'

'I control everything and spend excessive hours on work, which eats into my evenings and weekends and means that a lot of things outside of work don't get done. I get irritated quickly, which damages my relationships.'

By making a truthful, factual list of things that weren't working, looking directly at them and admitting the prices he paid for them, Patrick had forced himself to cut through the escape mechanisms that usually clouded his judgement. Underneath all the effort he put into keeping everything under control, he feared he was weak and unprofessional.

'Tell me,' I asked, 'is weakness a fact or an opinion?'

He paused.

'Is it tangible, can you touch it and see it?'

'No.'

'If it isn't physical, what is it?'

'Conceptual, I guess,' he said.

'Which means it's an opinion, right?'

'Yes,' he admitted.

'Whose opinion is it?'

'Mine.'

'Have you had this opinion about yourself for a few hours, or several decades?'

'The latter.'

'So you have been practising it. Is your opinion true?'

'No.'

'What would you call a thought that isn't true?' I asked.

'A mistake, I guess.'

'So you made a mistake and repeated it. Tell me, what are your qualities?' I asked him. 'Are you smart?'

'Yes.'

'Are you funny?'

'I like to think so,' he smiled.

'What else?'

We added 'creative', 'caring', 'sensitive' and 'good friend' to the list.

'Tell me, someone who is caring, sensitive, smart, funny and a good friend, does he need to work hard to prove he is good enough?' I asked.

'No.'

'What is the worst thing that could happen if you relinquished some control?'

'That someone would make a mistake.'

'By protecting your team members from making mistakes, are you supporting them to learn, or preventing them from learning?'

'I'm preventing them from growing.'

'So who is holding them back, you or them?'

'Me,' he laughed.

'Do you think your team members are capable of identifying and correcting their own mistakes?'

'Yes.'

'Can you know for certain whether a solution will work before you try it?'

'Not always, no. There is always some risk.'

'Can you create new opportunities and insights if you avoid taking risks?'

'No.'

'If you were a member of your team, would you dare to risk making a mistake?'

'I don't think so,' he admitted.

'By keeping everything under your control, what kind of example are you setting? Are you reassuring your team that it's OK to dare to try something new and that things can be corrected if necessary?'

'No.'

'And tell me,' I continued, 'if it's your controlling presence that ensures that everything goes smoothly, how much trust is there that your team can do things on their own?'

'Very little,' he recognised.

'So then you get stuck in a vicious circle. The more you control your team, the more you and the team depend on that control.'

He nodded. The point was clear.

Two weeks later, we came together for the programme completion day. Patrick looked excited and immediately raised his hand to share.

'I was really able to "read" my team members this week. Previously, if I heard someone asking slow and detailed questions, I saw it as lack of power and drive. Or even ignorance. It irritated me. This week, it was clear to me that this person had a certain communication style and was in the process of reflecting and trying to properly understand the issue. Just being able to see this made a huge difference, because I suddenly saw the care and the effort that person was putting into understanding the problem and it reassured me that the issue was being worked on. I also saw my own role in a totally different light. I understood that my job was to create the conditions for my team to do their job to the best of their ability. To dare to take risks and to feel confident about correcting mistakes where necessary. Once I understood that, it didn't even occur to me to get angry. I didn't need to try and control my anger; it just wasn't an issue anymore. I was also aware that raising my voice would make people with certain communication styles shut down and zone out. I know that this says nothing about that person's intelligence.'

'And what impact did you see that having?' I asked.

'As I did and spoke less, people started speaking up and taking more initiative. I have been going home at 5.00pm every day, but we have been getting more done. I know now that my biggest challenge is my ego. Sometimes I get scared and worry that we won't achieve our targets, but then I calm myself down by looking at the facts and focusing on the values I want to create in the team.'

Your fifth assignment: Problem solving

There is a whole culture around intelligence and what it is that makes someone 'smart'. Intelligence quota (IQ) tests check verbal comprehension, perceptual reasoning, working memory and processing speed. They are designed to gauge how well someone can use information and logic to answer questions or make predictions. Candidates for jobs in tech companies are generally expected to have a combination of technical knowledge, high IQ and communication skills. Most people assume being a good communicator means being good at talking, so people who are able to argue a point compellingly and convincingly tend to be regarded as intelligent. Meanwhile, there are no metrics for many of the qualities that are critical to getting things done with groups of people. These are not taught at school or university, nor are they measured in IQ and aptitude tests. The ability to read body language has no metric, nor is there one for humour and the ability to defuse tension; the ability to hear unspoken questions, to create a safe atmosphere, to listen carefully and pick up on subtle nuances, to see multiple sides of an argument. All of these competencies are key to working effectively with people, and yet none of them are measured.

In my experience, the picture a lot of people have of an intelligent person is someone who knows what they are talking about, who is able to argue their point logically and compellingly, who has things under control and who is able to deliver results quickly. As most people want to show they are smart enough for their job, these are the qualities most people think they need to practise and demonstrate.

The problem with this picture of intelligence is that it gives rise to a need to always be right. You start to believe you need to know your stuff and have things under control. And you start to invest more in keeping up appearances than being honest about what is not working and correcting it wisely. As a result, most people think it is more important to be right than to solve their problems and be happier and more effective.

This is why my partners and I have a specific definition of stupidity: a stupid person is someone who justifies their mistakes. Think about it for a moment: when you justify your mistakes, your motivation is not to correct the mistake but to defend it, meaning you will most likely repeat it. So actually a lot of highly educated people are stupid, because they are very good at justifying their mistakes.

ASSIGNMENT FIVE

Your fifth assignment is to pick one thing in your life that is not working and commit to addressing it. Don't make your ideas and beliefs about the 'right way' to go about it more important than your results. If you have been trying to solve this problem but haven't yet succeeded, this is an indication that you need to try something different.

Plan three practical actions or conversations to address this issue and carry them out in the next ten days.

SIX

How Logic Hijacked
Our Minds

If you cast your mind back, you can probably find a
memory of a hot day when you were relieved to stand
in the shade of a large leafy tree. Think back to that
sense of relief and gratitude and remember how your
senses took in the experience. The coolness, the rustling
of the leaves, the smell of the sap, the gentle breeze on
your hot neck and cheeks, a sense of gratitude for the
tree protecting you from the burning sun, the sheer size
of the trunk and the branches.

Intense experiences like this are not everyday occur-
rences. When they happen, they can be deeply moving –
watching the sun go down, going wild on the dance
floor, walking through a forest in the early morning

listening to the dawn chorus, making love while listening to the summer rain, walking through crunchy snow on a frosty morning. The reason moments like this have such an impact on us is that they overwhelm our senses, which is something we are not used to, as much of our life is spent at several degrees of separation from physical reality. This separation occurred in various stages as civilisations developed over thousands of years, and we didn't notice it happening.[16]

The first degree of separation came with the invention of language.[17] The very act of thinking and talking through language has a separating effect. The moment we say, 'That is an oak tree,' we place ourselves outside the unique real-time experience we had with a particular tree. The tree is no longer a unique sensory experience, but an example of a category of thing. By naming it, we step back from a sense of 'nowness' in which every moment is unique, into the realm of abstract concepts. When we talk about multiple trees, we take another step back into abstraction. The invention of numbers and counting increased our separation from unique moments in time and pulled us back into the realm of abstract concepts and thoughts, the realm of 'logical thinking'.

16   YN Harari, *Sapiens: A brief history of humankind* (Vintage, 2015)
17   C Eisenstein, *The Ascent of Humanity* (Panathea Productions, 2007)

Today, our minds are formed and trained in logical thinking. Logic relies on comparisons (A is more than, less than, or the same as B) and polarities, such as:

- Big exists because of small, beautiful exists because of ugly, smart exists because of stupid

- This carrot is larger than that carrot

- This student is more intelligent than that student

- This employee is more productive than that employee

- Susan is more successful than Jane

- He is more handsome than I am

Logical thinking has become the default. It is the system we use to judge everything, including ourselves and our lives, but it can leave us feeling empty and unhappy. Here's a thought experiment. Imagine that for the first time in your life you have planted some carrot seeds in the ground. You have tended and watered them and one day you see the fronds of the carrots poking up above the soil. Day by day, the green fronds of the carrot leaves grow higher and, as they do, you enjoy watching them wafting in the wind. Unfortunately, slugs eat most of the carrots and only one makes it to harvest time. You pull it out of the ground carefully, tugging firmly on the base of the leaves and feeling the root slip out of the soil. You don't, can't, compare that carrot to any other, you love it in its uniqueness. In that moment, you are free of logical thinking.

The problem with our habit of separating ourselves from the physical world through this mechanism of comparison and abstraction is that it destroys our appreciation for uniqueness. And with that, it destroys our sense of awe. When we hold a carrot that we have grown and harvested, we appreciate its unique shape, size and smell. We savour the moment when we pull it from the ground. It is a unique and personal experience. Buying twenty carrots from the supermarket is a far less awe-inspiring experience because the 'carrot' is reduced to an item that you have bought in a certain quantity. The carrot is no longer a unique experience; it is a commodity. The exact size or smell of each of the twenty carrots is not important. That is the nature of commodities – each unit can be exchanged for another. If you order 10 kg of fresh ripe strawberries, it doesn't matter which strawberries you receive and where they were grown. All that matters is the quantity.

If you are a parent, think back to when your child was born. You will have been filled with an appreciation of the sacredness of human life. You wouldn't have compared your child – you fell in love with the unique human being that they are. You will have been in awe of the unique moment and of the whole experience of becoming a parent. You continue to love your child unconditionally.

Most of our waking lives, though, are spent in the default mode of logical thinking and we don't appreciate the uniqueness of each moment. In this mode, we experience most things – like time, strawberries, people – in quantities, the same way we measure electricity and data. We commoditise life, and this influences how we experience everything, including the relationship we have with ourselves. Logic compartmentalises unique experiences and turns them into recognisable categories and quantities. It turns us into detached observers of experiences that would fill us with awe and wonder if only we were able to be present in the uniqueness of the moment. It transforms the unique and sacred into the mechanical and profane.

Every time you say, 'I should have done that,' you contemplate a hypothetical direction you didn't take. That's an abstraction. You are removing yourself from your reality. You do it when you compare yourself with others. You do it every time you think, 'I should ...' This is how you kill your soul and lose yourself.

I should note that feelings are also logical. If you smile at me, I feel happy. If you complain to me, I feel irritated. If you criticise me, I feel down. If A, then B. If C, then D. A lot of people see feelings as the opposite of rational thinking, but they follow the same logic.

Don't get me wrong, logical thought is an incredible and brilliant tool. It has been responsible for the

THE GEEK'S GUIDE TO WORK

staggering steps forward humans have made. It started with the evolution of a complex grammar and syntax which allowed us to communicate with each other about events in other places and at other moments in time. Our ability to conceptualise is what has allowed us to tell stories, capture each other's imaginations and get large numbers of people to collaborate in shared endeavours.[18]

The solution is not to turn the clocks back, return to nature and pretend we don't have logical minds. The ability to think at this level of complexity is a miracle of evolution. The point is that your mind is programmed with software called logic, which has taken over; it is sometimes perfect for the job, but is often disturbing and destructive. The question you want to ask yourself is, how can you increase your mastery of this software (including your ability to turn it on and off when needed) so that it supports you to get your life really working? So that it makes you happy, supports your relationships, heightens your sensitivity to the sacredness of life and supports you to care for the world you live in?

Case study: Emmanuel

I met Emmanuel when I was doing a team session with a group of thirty individuals from a tech company

---

18   YN Harari, *Sapiens: A brief history of humankind* (Vintage, 2015)

that built banking websites. In the first session, they introduced themselves one by one, including what was not working in their professional situation. As we went round the group, there were two recurring themes, encapsulated in the quotes below:

1. 'There is very little pride internally about what we are doing. The company presents itself to the outside world as a fantastic place to work, but internally people aren't proud of what they do.'

2. 'There is an impatience to the way we run briefings and meetings, so that critical questions on specific details get swept aside. We don't spend enough time thinking things through thoroughly.'

As the morning progressed and more members of the team introduced themselves, these two points came up again and again in different ways. Some of the longer-serving team members reported that this had been going on for several years. I challenged them on this.

'So you noticed that there was a particular culture, and that it didn't work for you. What did you do about it?' I asked.

Many of them had complained to their managers, and some had tried to address the subject with other team members, but all had given up. Three of the partici-pants in the group asked me to coach them after that session. One of them, Emmanuel, approached me with a fiery look in his eyes. 'This really makes sense,' he said. 'I have a lot of issues I want to work out. I want more of this, can you help me?'

He loved his work, but several tense relationships with colleagues were making his life difficult. In our first session, he laid out the situation in his team, including the various roles and responsibilities, and where the tensions were. 'Let's zoom in on one of these tense relationships,' I suggested. 'Describe to me what a typical tense situation would look like.'

'The engineer in my team never keeps to his agreements,' he explained. 'It's all very jovial and cosy, and he talks a lot, but I'm fed up with the fact that every time we agree anything, he forgets, is too late, or someone has to remind him.'

'What is his communication style?' I asked (we had learned about and practised communication styles in the programme).

'He had a dominant informal style. I had forgotten about the styles.'

'Do you talk to him in that communication style?' I asked.

'No.'

'Then your homework this week is to talk to him in the dominant informal style.'

Emmanuel was formal and business-like in his communication style, so this task meant approaching conversations with the engineer in a more jovial way, with more stories and personal contact. Less email, more face-to-face. We then proceeded to look at the communication styles of all the people he had tension with, and I tasked him with practising these communication styles, to change his energy and the level of formality or informality in his communication.

The next week he came in smiling. He had practised and he'd had a great conversation with the engineer, in which he felt they really got each other. He didn't have to raise the point about missing deadlines, 'Because he brought it up himself, he apologised and promised that at the next meeting he would be on time.'

The miraculous thing was, by focusing on practising the communication style and getting on the wavelength of the person he was having issues with, many of the difficult subjects Emmanuel had avoided discussing with his colleagues came up organically. Then I asked him what else was bothering him at work. 'I don't know what it is,' he said, 'but something is not right. I love my job, this company is my home, but I am fed up with how negative and spoiled some people are.'

'Which people?' I asked. 'The engineer?'

'No, he's a good guy. He's doing his best.' We went through every person in the team and examined the relationship he had with each of them, looking at it through the filter of each person's communication style. It was to be expected that those with passive formal styles were getting on with things quietly. It would be a worrying sign if they weren't showing interest by asking questions, or had gone silent in meetings, but this wasn't the case.

'So, if it's not the team, what is it that is bothering you?' I asked.

'Now I see it,' he said. 'It's the fact that it's not clear who is leading the team, whether it's me or Tony.' He explained that he was jointly responsible for the team together with a colleague called Tony. It was an interim solution until a definitive tribe leader had been assigned. Things had just evolved that way, but Emmanuel was not comfortable with it.

'We both have the title of tribe leader, but to be honest it's annoying me that he isn't doing anything at all to support the team. He is always away on business trips. He wants to be included in the updates, but when he is here all he does is lecture the team on what they should be doing, which stresses everyone out. He undoes all the good work I'm doing. We are currently both being considered for the tribe leader position. I think I deserve it more.'

For a moment he looked shocked at his own honesty. 'Aha, so that's it,' I said. 'At least now you have identified the source of your annoyance, you know what it is and what it isn't. So what are you going to do about it?'

He considered this for a moment. 'I'm going to address it with my manager in our next meeting,' he said. 'I am going to be clear with her that I want that position.'

'Have you considered having a conversation with Tony?'

'Yes,' said Emmanuel. 'I am going to have a straight conversation with him too.'

In our session two weeks later, he had spoken to his manager and it was clear that the work he was doing with the team was seen and appreciated. He had also had a short conversation with Tony, which had been difficult, and Tony had not agreed with him.

In the three months that followed, he focused on being there for the team when they needed him, practising communication styles and creating a safe atmosphere by sharing his own mistakes, insights, challenges and progress. Encouraging his team to dare to make their own calls and learn from both their victories and their mistakes, and getting them to identify and recognise the progress they were making.

Your sixth assignment: Dissecting negative thoughts

The ego loves chewing on stories that give it a hit of self-righteousness. It loves emotional highs, and nothing beats indignation (or outrage) as the source. It sounds counterproductive, and it is, but we love to feel indignant. We can spend hours, days, even years of our short lives feeling angry or incredulous about situations at work, feeding our outrage with stories about unfairness, about blame, about misunderstandings. All the while, we forget that this anger is eating away at our happiness and relationships.

You pay a heavy price for anger. Often the price is disguised. Maybe your two-year-old is getting used to you being an angry person. Maybe you have been thinking, 'Is this it?' for the past five years. Maybe you are becoming cynical and flippant. Or maybe you can't let your hair down without alcohol and the only time you are yourself is when you are on holiday. You may have been passed over for a promotion, you might have lost a job, or a relationship. The chances are that, instead of examining the stories you tell, you told yourself, 'That's life. Shit happens,' or, 'It's just my luck.'

You want to be careful with the stories you tell. You need to untangle them, pull them apart and separate the truth from fiction. The way to do this is by learning to identify the separate elements present in any story: facts, thoughts and feelings. Ask yourself, 'What actually happened?' and then, 'What are my thoughts about those facts?' Remember, your thoughts are only thoughts. Your ego will do its best to tell you they are the truth, but they are just thoughts. You need to be accurate and look closely at the thoughts within the thoughts; this will cast a lot of light on what you are feeling. It will become clear which thoughts generated which feelings. This is the process of gaining clarity.

ASSIGNMENT SIX

In the coming twelve hours, as soon as you notice any negative feeling arise, take yourself off to somewhere you can be alone. Then work through the following three steps:

1. Give the feeling a one-word description.
2. Look for the specific thought that created the feeling. For example, 'I shouldn't have...', or, 'I should have...', or, 'It was a shame that...'
3. Identify the event that triggered the thought. For example, a message came up on your phone, or someone walked past, which reminded you of something.

Write these down and note that it was simply a thought that created the feeling.

Summary: Clarity

- Our happiness is strongly influenced by the expectations we have of ourselves. All of us have an internal dialogue going on, in which our expectations influence what we think about our factual reality. Those thoughts in turn influence our feelings, which then colour our further thoughts. Untangling thoughts, facts and feelings allows you to act on what you can change and accept what you can't.

- We have all developed ways of avoiding looking at reality. Most people are experts in using mental escape mechanisms to get away with counterproductive behaviour. Untangling your thinking starts with identifying and deactivating what you are avoiding.

- Anger is not a problem; it is a habit you may have got accustomed to. Admitting that anger has benefits as well as costs will show you that you control it more than you think.

- There is a disempowering story in our culture that intelligence is about knowing things and being right, which leads a lot of professionals to do their best to avoid mistakes. Real intelligence is the ability to get things working. Give yourself permission to try things out and risk getting a different result than planned – and be proud of yourself for doing so.

- Our logical mind works through comparison, which often leaves us dissatisfied and unhappy. Western culture values logical thinking highly. While it is a powerful instrument for solving logistical and mathematical problems, logical thinking numbs our sensitivity and our sense of joy and wonderment.

- The ego likes to chew on stories of indignation and anger that give us emotional highs.

Don't forget to take the Inspiring Leader Questionnaire at https://juliasullivan.scoreapp.com when you get to the end of the book. You will find out how you currently rate against the HACCA model and get practical insights you can use straight away.

PART FOUR
COURAGE

The willingness to put ourselves in vulnerable situations

M any people are aware of the prices of modern life: of the way we are separated from what is real and how we make our lives difficult with our thinking. But very few people look for a satisfactory solution. OK, that's not entirely true. Many do look for a solution, but nearly all of them search for something that fits their thinking. They match possible solutions against their logic, with its symbols and comparisons, based on past experience. It's a process of assessing new information using an existing value system – and thinking it will work.

It's understandable, and we all do it. We have all developed finely calibrated antennae with which we filter out the unreasonable and the ridiculous and protect ourselves from deceivers. We would be naïve not to. But ultimately what this process does is filter out anything which has no place in (or perhaps threatens) the old thinking, leaving us with more of what we had. Unsurprisingly, the same old problems keep returning.

Most people associate courage with doing things that scare them, like public speaking or parachuting. But that kind of fear – when we go weak at the knees, get sweaty palms and start shaking – is simply a physical reaction to our thinking, which at those moments is firing on all cylinders, running through various scenarios of things that could go wrong. This sends a rush of adrenaline through our body, putting it on high alert. It's a physiological process.

There is another form of fear that doesn't send our body into high alert and has no physical symptoms. This fear arises when we say we want to do something, and we think we mean it, but then we don't do it. Why don't we do it? There is often no real reason. There is nothing stopping us, no one telling us not to, no physical obstacles. Yet still, we don't do it. Meanwhile, we continue thinking. That incessant internal dialogue is going on all the time, and it speaks in the language and syntax it was brought up with. It uses the logic it was taught. The result of all that thinking is that we don't take the step we said we wanted to take. This can go on for days, weeks, months or years. For many people, it lasts a lifetime.

From the outside, courage is when we dare to do something scary like horse riding, bungee jumping or giving a presentation to a large auditorium of people. But courage on the inside is when we dare to do something that our wiser self tells us we should do, while our chattering logic tries to talk us out of it.

SEVEN

Say Goodbye To Your Comfort Zone

Why do most people find it so difficult to do something as simple as admitting they don't have an answer, or that something is not working? Why do so many people put themselves under so much pressure to pretend they have everything under control, rather than asking for help? Why do most people prefer to stick to what they know and defend the stories they tell themselves – including those that make them feel down?

The answer can be best summarised in a well-known expression: 'Better the devil you know than the devil you don't.' Most people prefer to stick with what they know, even if it is making their life difficult and unpleasant, rather than try something unfamiliar that could make them happier and more successful.

You are accustomed to your ways of thinking and reacting, and you are used to the hopes and fears that go with them. This is what the comfort zone is. It isn't comfortable, but you are so used to the discomfort that it has become part of your life and you don't recognise it as discomfort anymore. What is keeping you there? The internal library of thoughts, concepts and stories that you have accumulated over the years that make up your inner world. You are unaware of most of these stories because they are such a fundamental part of your picture of reality that you take them for granted. You are strongly attached to this library of thoughts and stories because it creates your identity, it tells you that you know who you are.

Your need to prove you are good enough by pretending you are smarter, kinder or more in control than you fear you are – that's your comfort zone. It comes at a cost in terms of energy and stress, and the life it necessitates sometimes feels flat and empty. It's so familiar that you think it is who you are; you don't admit, or even see, the discomfort you are in. Meanwhile, life is changing around you at a rapid rate and has a habit of confronting you with situations that 'you' are not prepared to handle. When life becomes threatening, 'you' react by doing more of what you're used to. That could be blaming others. It could be blaming yourself. It could be walking away. It could be putting yourself under more pressure. It could be pretending not to care. It could be all sorts of behaviours. Your comfort zone compels you to do more of the only thing it knows, trapping you in more of the same.

Meanwhile, the people around you are on the receiving end of all that ineffectual effort, and they will not react kindly. They will either stop telling you their truth and disengage or tell it more aggressively. Your relationship with yourself will also suffer as your self-confidence dwindles.

Your personal logic is a key part of your comfort zone, but it is such a deep-rooted part of you that you have never stopped to think about it. It's like forgetting you are wearing a pair of sunglasses: you look outside and everything appears dark and gloomy; you don't realise your view is coloured by your dark lenses.

You have probably got used to various things in your life not working, so that you don't see the problems anymore. A great first step to escaping your (dis)comfort zone is daring to do something that will seriously challenge your thinking.

Case study: Stefano

Stefano was a CEO in his late forties. During a training task he had witnessed the way the leader in one of the games was giving directions and telling people what to do, kindly but resolutely cutting off objections in the name of efficiency.

Stefano noticed that the approach created pressure in the group. Some people pushed harder, became more assertive, interrupting more and listening less, while others sat back and became hesitant to the point of disengaging. At the end of the game, some of them shared that they felt stupid and assumed others understood the game better than they did. They felt they didn't understand the game well enough to say anything, so kept quiet. They could no longer follow the discussion and felt out of their depth.

Stefano stood up to share his view on how the game had been run. 'I recognise a lot in how Leader X led this game. This is how I lead my company and my family. I have clear ideas about the way things should be done,' he said, 'and I make sure things are done that way.' He talked about his drive to become successful, about the pressure he had felt to be right and to know what he was talking about, and about how it had alienated some of his co-workers.

'I was so concerned about the business and fixated on the idea that I needed to be strong enough, smart enough and decisive enough to lead it well. I was a talker, talking all the time. Explaining how things worked, trying to show that I knew what I was talking about. Telling people what was important and what wasn't. I couldn't stand what I perceived to be stupidity and felt it was important I show people what was right.

I would spend a lot of time advising my co-workers too, telling them how to approach problems. I felt it was my role as the director. But I noticed that some of my managers didn't talk a lot. I didn't know what was going on. I thought they were insecure and needed encouraging and advising. Now I see that they were probably tired of my lectures. They had given up. They would let my words wash over them.'

'How was that for you, feeling that the success of the company rested solely on your shoulders and that it was up to you to motivate everyone?' I asked.

'Exhausting. Last year the company almost went bankrupt. I hardly slept. I was worried sick, and it felt pretty lonely. I didn't have anyone to share my worries with. I felt I needed a stiff upper lip and to keep the morale up.'

'What about at home? Were you different there?' I asked.

'I did the same thing. I would talk and talk. I wanted my children to grow up knowing what was important, what was going on the world. I wanted things in our family to work and I would give them advice.'

'How was that for your partner?'

'It nearly broke our marriage. We drifted apart.'

'What did you make more important, your relationship with your partner, or your opinions and need to be right?'

'My opinions. It wasn't my intention, I genuinely thought I was doing the right thing, but our relationship suffered. I lost touch with her.'

'When you as a leader think you should know everything and you have to be right, what kind of culture do you create? Will you have employees who can think and stand on their own feet, or obedient followers who simply take your word for it?'

'I create obedience. I don't teach people to think for themselves.'

'That sounds like a waste of the intelligence in your team, like you could just as well replace them with robots.'

I asked him what his fear had been all that time and he replied, 'I always thought a leader needed to know what they were talking about. I could never admit I was wrong. I was afraid of losing authority and respect.'

Once he had articulated this, he paused. There was a moment's silence while his words sunk in. He'd realised that his fear had been based on a false story. His face relaxed. In the days that followed, he was milder. He listened carefully and thoughtfully as other people shared.

The following week we returned for the completion evening, and I asked him how the week had been.

'I had some great conversations with my managers. I shared with them; I was open, much more so than I was before. They told me I looked relaxed, and I got so many compliments. I've noticed a difference in my management team. They are more relaxed, they speak up more, there is more humour. My style of leadership has changed. Instead of wanting to prove I know things, I am more aware of creating the conditions for my managers to grow and be successful.'

Your seventh assignment: Challenging your comfort zone

There is a misconception about the comfort zone, which is that people think it has to do with our external environment and how we behave in it. But the comfort zone is as much about our inner world – about the thinking habits and patterns that have become part of our reality. Another misconception is that the comfort zone is where we feel comfortable. Let me be clear: the only comfortable thing about the comfort zone is its familiarity. If you are accustomed to feeling down, that is your comfort zone. If you are used to feeling impatient, that's your comfort zone. You may have become accustomed to all kinds of counterproductive states of mind – jealousy, anger, numbness, boredom, guilt, a chronic sense of not being good enough, and many more.

Remember that everything has a price and a benefit. If your thinking habits make you feel bad, and if you notice that you feel bad and don't break the pattern, this means it must benefit you in some way.

Some of these moods, such as generally feeling down, give us permission to be mentally lazy. When we are feeling blue, we are not in the mood to challenge ourselves. Other forms of negativity, like anger and irritation, keep people at arm's length, which can be a benefit. It can be convenient not to have to listen to input we don't want to hear. It can also be a way of forcing others to do what we want, so it's a form of domination and control. The biggest benefit is that no one can argue with us because, 'Hey, this is just the way I feel,' so we are always right.

ASSIGNMENT SEVEN

Your seventh assignment is to reflect on a situation that is bothering you. When you have one in mind, ask yourself:

- What am I not doing to solve it?
- How have I been avoiding solving it?
- What is the price of not solving it?
- What is the benefit of not solving it?

EIGHT

Dare To Go Beyond Your Image

French philosopher Jean Paul Sartre famously included the phrase 'Hell is other people' in his play *No Exit*.[19] The truth about living and working with other people is that they have minds we can't control; they are constantly thinking and forming opinions. We are aware of this, and we assume that they are thinking things about us, because we drive ourselves crazy with our own opinions and stories about ourselves. Then, as if we're in a hall of mirrors, we worry about what we *think* other people are thinking about us. Let me repeat that. We create an illusion that other people think

---

19 J-P Sartre, *No Exit and Other Plays*, translated by L Abel (Vintage, 1989)

things about us, then we get worried about what the opinions that we have invented for them are. There is a word for this phenomenon: image.

If you have ever hesitated to ask a question for fear of sounding stupid, your image had you. If you have ever not asked for a date with someone you fancied, your image had you. If you have ever gone along with a plan you didn't agree with for fear of sounding negative, your image got you. 'But Julia,' you might object, 'it is likely that my manager has an opinion about me and that it's not all positive.' The more you think about it, the more you will believe the negative things that you *think* your manager is thinking. The point is not whether it is likely that they have an opinion about you. The point is that, if you haven't asked what your manager thinks, those negative thoughts remain your own projection. They weigh heavily on you. They make you self-conscious, kill your spontaneity and increase your self-doubt.

The more importance you place on opinions in general, the more likely you are to do this. The more critical and judgemental you are, the more likely you are to be concerned about what others may think about you, the more trapped you become by your image. You worry whether your shoes and clothes are cool enough, whether your holidays are interesting enough, whether you are funny enough, whether your house is nice enough.

You compare, judge and form opinions on a regular basis. Measuring and comparing one person with another is part of the operating system of your thinking. You do it without noticing. Every second, you are observing the people and events around you – who to take seriously and who not to, who is successful and who is not. In your logically trained mind, your worth is dependent on being more than or equal to the people around you. We are continuously checking our position in the pecking order of our various groups. Our minds observe and interpret every comment, every move, every facial expression, every bodily signal. There is a continuous process going on, whether we like it or not, in which we assess where we stand in comparison to others. 'Am I as smart or funny (or confident, or successful) as this person?' We make our value dependent on others, which destroys our sense of our unique, inherent worth.

You are judging your actions and yourself continuously, and so you assume that others are judging you just as mercilessly. Your comfort zone has you trapped and your concern about what others may think about you dominates your life.

Case study: Carla

Carla, thirty-five, was a leader in a fintech company that had grown from 500 to 1,000 people over two years.

Her manager had approached me to provide coaching because she was struggling in her role.

In our intake meeting, Carla explained to me that there were five product teams in her 'tribe' of twenty-five, and there was tension between some of the leaders. One of the issues was competition for capacity and resources, she explained. For example, one of the product owners had recently snapped up a disproportionate chunk of developers' hours for his team's project, which left the other teams struggling and understaffed. This was not unusual in the company, she explained, it was generally seen as healthy competition.

But Carla felt that the atmosphere in the tribe was tense and she wanted to do something to create more positivity. She'd had the idea to set up a monthly tribe meeting on the last Friday of the month and to invite each team to share their biggest successes of the month. They had pushed the table football back so that they could fit the whole team in the coffee area and set up a screen so that they could show films and photos. She'd been excited.

The team arrived in dribs and drabs, floating around the coffee area, fixing their drinks and checking their phones. A couple of latecomers sent a ripple of laughs and shrugs through the room, an expectant quiet descended on the group and they all looked at Carla.

She thanked the team for supporting the initiative and told them she was confident there would be no shortage of successes to share. Then she sat down. And the group fell silent.

After a few coughs, one of the team leaders stood up and told the group that their presentation to the client the previous week had gone well. There had been some concerns raised by the clients, but now it looked like a serious escalation had been diverted. The group clapped. And then again there was silence.

A developer reported that they were on track with their project. Applause. Then silence.

Someone else stood up and announced that his youngest team member had turned thirty. Everyone laughed and clapped. Then the group started to get impatient, and Carla finished the meeting soon after. She was disappointed. Why wasn't the team playing along?

In the session we had the next week, we spoke about it. 'Have you considered that some of the team may feel manipulated because you only asked for the positive stories?' I asked her.

'No, I hadn't thought of that,' she said. 'Do you know, some of them told me they thought it was "too American". I never really looked at it that way.'

'When you ask a group to "be positive", what you're really saying is, "I don't want to hear any negativity." In a team in which there is tension or differences of opinion, that is going to create a lot of resistance,' I explained.

Carla and I had a conversation in which she told me how, for the previous five years or so, she had been working hard and enthusiastically to motivate her team. She had given compliments, encouraged people to speak up, spoken about the importance of bringing your whole self to your job, compiled a library of inspirational books and changed the onboarding process. You name it, she'd done it. She had been working incredibly hard. Yet again and again she had faced lukewarm reactions from team members who smiled, expressed appreciation and then went back to their work. What she had hoped to achieve never materialised; in her eyes, none of them had become the inspiring partners she was looking for.

She decided to stop the 'Success of the month' meetings. Instead, she set up individual monthly meetings with the other four team leaders in her tribe, in which she invited them to be truthful on three topics:

1. **Progress on the projects:** Were the KPIs being met? Where were the bottlenecks?

2. **Quality of cooperation in the team:** Were the conversations that needed to happen, happening? Were people showing up? Was there ownership, or was there blame? Were people aware of their progress? Was there a sense of pride around how challenges were being handled?

3. **Their communication with themselves:**
   Were they clear on their priorities? Were they
   approaching challenges with the values they
   considered important? Were they criticising
   themselves for their mistakes, or were they
   praising themselves for the risks and initiative
   they took? Were they learning lessons from their
   mistakes?

On all three of these levels, she wanted to know what
was going well, what wasn't and what suggestions they
had moving forward.

The moment Carla replaced the previous group meetings with the one-on-ones with the team leaders, she
sensed a change of energy in the team. The four team
leaders stopped resisting her, felt they were being
taken more seriously and began to address problems
proactively and with more maturity. Meanwhile, Carla
had more time. She saw the team leaders stepping up
to take ownership and she stopped chasing them, simply making herself available for them if they needed
support.

In the beginning, she found this scary, because it meant
stepping back and doing less, which initially felt like
giving up control. After a few weeks, however, she
started to enjoy being less stressed. Her days were no
longer filled with firefighting, and she had space to look
around, observe what was happening and decide when
to keep quiet and when to offer support.

Your eighth assignment: Noticing where you hold back

In the last few decades, whole communities of thinkers have been re-examining our relationship with nature in light of the climate crisis. Many have argued that the concept of a 'relationship with nature' itself is wrong, as it rests on the premise that we stand outside of nature. We don't have a relationship with nature, we *are* nature, they point out. Somewhere down the line, though, we seem to have forgotten this.

One of the lines of thinking that has gained traction is the story of separation, as we touched on earlier. We see ourselves as separate from nature. During the Enlightenment, scientists and thinkers set out to translate nature into numbers. The assumption was that if we could measure everything, we would achieve perfect understanding and perfect control. This has informed the modern scientific method, which essentially involves converting things into numbers,[20] and then using mathematical equations to convert these numbers into other numbers, at increasing levels of abstraction.

Another key thinker who has informed the way we perceive and understand the world – and was known in his time as 'the most intelligent man in the world' – is

---

20 C Eisenstein, *The Ascent of Humanity* (Panathea Productions, 2007)

René Descartes.[21] The story goes that on a freezing cold winter some 400 years ago, a crowd of eager students in waistcoats had crammed into the auditorium of Utrecht University, Holland, to hear him speak. Allegedly, he walked in with a dog, who lay on the stage while Descartes explained the workings of nature as he would the mechanics of a clock. Then, with a swing of his boot, he kicked the dog in the belly. The audience were horrified as the dog howled. 'You think what you are seeing is pain,' Descartes allegedly said, as if he were revealing the key to the universe, 'but what you are seeing is merely a physical reflex. Animals don't feel pain. Humans are exceptional. We are chosen. And not only is every other creature of inferior intelligence, but no other creatures have emotions, thoughts, or even the capacity for physical sensations.'

Descartes, like many brilliant thinkers of the time, including Newton and Galileo, was working from the school of thought developed by the Ancient Greeks some 1,500 years earlier. It was the Greeks who came up with the idea that the universe is bound by a set of fixed 'ultimate truths' and that only through a process of highly rational objective thinking could one hope to discover these truths.[22] Getting to the ultimate truth of nature meant casting your focus 'out there', using your mind to break things down into categories and

21 G Ferguson, *Eight Master Lessons of Nature* (Penguin, 2019)
22 E Hall, *The Ancient Greeks: Ten ways they shaped the modern world* (Random House, 2006)

component parts. That approach, which Descartes underpinned with mathematics, quickly ceased to be seen as a theory or intellectual story, and was accepted as truth. If you couldn't establish the clear physical boundaries of a thing, hold it outside yourself, fixed in time and space, then it didn't exist. In the 1600s, Galileo invented the experimental method, based on evidence and calculation.[23] The Greeks before him were using the technologies of language and counting, which had been developed thousands of years previously, to conceptualise and understand the world.

You are a child of a culture that was shaped by thinkers such as Newton, Galileo and Descartes, who in turn were influenced by the likes of Archimedes, Aristotle and Plato. You have them to thank for the way you were taught to think, what you were taught about intelligence and the metrics you use to quantify life. It also shouldn't be forgotten that the scientific academy that was born during the Enlightenment banned Jews, women and black people from participating. The Royal Society in London was founded in 1660 and first admitted a woman in 1900.[24] Similarly, women had been excluded from the scientific and political arena in Ancient Greece.[25] The art of thinking evolved and

23 A Zanatta et al, 'Galileo Galilei: Science vs. faith', *Global Cardiology Science and Practice*, 2/10 (2017), www.ncbi.nlm.nih.gov/pmc/articles/PMC5871402, accessed September 2021
24 R Holmes, 'The Royal Society's lost women scientists', *The Guardian* (21 November 2010), www.theguardian.com/science/2010/nov/21/royal-society-lost-women-scientists, accessed September 2021
25 S Blundell, *Women in Ancient Greece* (Harvard University Press, 1995)

was developed over the course of nearly 3,000 years by a small part of the population, yet the narratives it gave birth to were widely accepted and remained unquestioned for a long time.

ASSIGNMENT EIGHT

The first step in releasing the grip of your logical mind, and its need to compare and judge, is to identify it. Over the next forty-eight hours, make a note of every time you hesitate or fail to do or say something you want to because of fear of what someone may think.

Summary:
Courage

- Most people are vaguely aware of the prices of modern life. Those who look for solutions usually seek approaches that fit their existing concepts. In doing so, they perpetuate the same way of thinking that gave rise to the problem in the first place.

- There are two kinds of fear: fear of something specific, which sparks a physiological reaction, and fear of taking action, which has no symptoms. The only indication of the latter is that we want something but do nothing to obtain it.

- The term 'comfort zone' refers to your way of thinking and reacting. The comfort zone can be an uncomfortable place and often has a high price.

THE GEEK'S GUIDE TO WORK

You become so used to the discomfort that you no longer recognise it, and think, 'That's life.'

- Life is dynamic and changes all the time, which means we are regularly confronted with the unfamiliar, and situations that make us doubt ourselves. If we don't challenge ourselves to find new ways of approaching life, we return to the familiar default but work harder, meaning the prices we pay increase.

- The more judgemental we are in general, the more likely we are to judge ourselves and worry about the opinions of others. This phenomenon is part of the perpetual process of comparison our logical thinking is engaged in. The first step towards overcoming this is to notice and name it.

- Courage is the willingness to go beyond our image and act despite fear of what others might think.

PART FIVE
AUTHENTICITY

When we lead our lives according to our natural values

Recently, it has become fashionable to 'just be yourself.' It's an epithet that frequently appears in motivational quotes on social media, and in the past ten years various schools of management have also adopted the idea. But this is a naïve approach, as it ignores the reality that our minds have been hijacked by numerous forces, such as logic, ego and fear, which give rise to thoughts that make us unhappy and react in ways we later regret.

Being authentic is about learning to be the person we could be without fear and ego. It is about identifying them, outsmarting them, standing above them and being wiser. This is the practice of self-awareness.

Self-awareness is a hugely exciting and satisfying art that will develop your clarity of thinking, courage, presence of mind, integrity and sensitivity. It is the art of learning to be the person you want to be in all areas of your life, without pretending or hiding anything. It is the most important education anyone can give themselves.

Authenticity is living according to your natural values. Why natural? This is to overcome a trick of the mind, because there is a high chance that when you choose values to live your life by, you are unwittingly led by fear. For example, if you have a history of working for bosses who micro-manage, the values of freedom and respect will be high on your list, simply as a reaction to your past. If you have a fear of being poor, material success might be one of your values. There is nothing wrong with freedom, respect or material success, but choosing values to prove you are good enough will only increase your fear of failure.

Your natural values are the ones you would choose to live by if you had nothing to prove, nothing to fear and nothing to put straight.

NINE

Make Your Choice, Pay The Price And Enjoy The Fruits

'Nature abhors a vacuum,' a phrase often attributed to Aristotle, applies not only to the physical world, but to our thinking too.[26] We all have times when we get up and look forward to an empty day just free-wheeling...and then the day fills up with all sorts of chores. Or a week off, during which we don't get round to picking up any of the books we said we would read. It's just how it goes. If we don't have a plan, life makes

---

26 F Wilczek, 'What is space?', *MIT Physics Annual 2009* (MIT Press, 2009)

plans for us. We go where life takes us, like tumbleweed blown down a road.

There are times when this works out fine and we are happy to trundle along with whatever life has in store. Sometimes, though, we look back and wonder why we didn't make better use of our time – why we didn't set up that company while the concept was hot, why we didn't date and find a partner before we were too old to have kids, why we didn't invest while house prices were low, why we didn't study for that degree when we had the time. It's easy to spot the 'right path' in retrospect, but guilt and regret are bad teachers and lead to bitterness.

These days, you can't swipe a smartphone screen without hearing about goal setting and planning and how you too could be taking your life to the next level. 'Do you want to be as successful as these smiling entrepreneurs?' Instagram asks. 'Dare to set challenging goals and go for them!' They tell you, 'It's time to stop being lazy. Get off your couch, get yourself in gear and find the passion and drive in your life!' Challenges and stories like these flood social media, but hey, what's wrong with being comfortable on the couch?

These narratives about drive, success and focus can get tiring and depressing. They sound loud and self-congratulatory. They begin to prompt a different reaction to the one they're seeking. 'I'm happy; leave me alone. I don't need you telling me how great you are to spur me into action. I don't need your goal setting and planning!'

In the story of separation, goal setting and planning are tools that sit outside ourselves. They are the bridles and saddles for our wild horses. They impose discipline and focus on our chaotic, undisciplined and unrefined nature. And the hidden message we often hear when people suggest we should set clear goals and plan better is that who we are now is not good enough.

In the story of connectedness, when we admit that we are part of nature, it becomes clear that every cell and organ in our body works with an incredible level of discipline, precision and harmony. If you observe a child learning to walk, how she first practises her balance until she trusts it, then observes her environment until she sees a suitable opportunity. How she takes a step and falls, how she repeats the procedure time and time again, finetuning and correcting it so that every attempt is better than the last. There is no question that drive, focus, self-discipline and determination are qualities that we inherently possess in more than sufficient quantities.

As we reach adulthood and go out into the world, into the noise and the surfeit of possibilities, we are free to choose our direction in life. It is no longer always predetermined by the place we were born or the profession of our parents. We can choose almost anything. We can be born to a family of bakers in North Dakota and become a management consultant in Tokyo. The possibilities are endless. If we are not careful, this surfeit of possibilities can be bad for our mental health. Like going into a bar and ordering every drink they have, we can become intoxicated by the wealth of choices available. Our minds start spinning and we fall into a stupor, paralysed by indecision in the face of all the things we could be doing. Our natural ability to focus and apply ourselves evaporates, days and weeks fill up, months and years pass, leaving us with a low-grade nausea, a feeling of 'Is this it?'

When we are in this state, pulled in every direction by infinite possibilities, it can make us miserable. We also have lots of time to think – about everything and everyone. Things bother us. We can get upset and cross about something someone the other side of the world said about someone we have never heard of. We can get so upset that it spoils our day, even our whole week. We read the news and we feel concerned, guilty and angry about the state of the world and the way humans are. When we are in this state of limbo and indecision, we squander our natural ability to concentrate and focus and open our thinking to all the negativity it can find to chew on. Because our minds get bored. The mind likes to be at work, and if you don't give it a clear task, it will mull over anything it can find.

Seen within this context, goal setting and planning are not about disciplining and improving your chaotic and unruly self, but about enabling yourself to choose, to quieten down, to consciously turn away from the noise and the infinite possibilities around you and pursue a direction you have chosen. Every choice we make has consequences. Choosing one direction rules out another. Choosing to get pregnant means you won't be doing that 200 km hike through the mountains this year. Many people avoid making choices because they don't want to live with the consequences, but this is simply choosing to sit on the fence. You can't win that way, because you can't enjoy the fruits of a plan without paying the price for it. Making a wholehearted choice involves being aware of and accepting its consequences.

The critical word here is 'choice'. Most people don't stop to ask themselves what they want from life. A lot of people choose a profession or a direction of study, but in many cases, while they think this is a free choice, it is heavily influenced by what they think they *should* choose. They are afraid of disappointing their family or scared of what their friends will think. Very few people stop to ask themselves about the values they have inherited and whether those values truly make them happy. This means that a lot of people end up making life choices that make them unhappy.

Case study: Sofia

Sofia was an experienced compliance officer in her early forties working for a fast-growing scale-up. She

THE GEEK'S GUIDE TO WORK

was a busy woman; every morning when she opened her mailbox there would be nine or ten new queries, each of which required serious attention, and throughout the day more questions and requests for help would stream in.

Sofia was a conscientious person and did her best to answer each query thoroughly. Sometimes they were legal questions about potential scenarios the company had not faced before; others were about routine procedures that were detailed in the company's compliance handbook. As the individuals asking were often new to the company and didn't know where to find the information, Sofia would take the time to explain and point them in the right direction. The problem was that the company was growing. This meant that increasing numbers of young ambitious newbies were messaging her and impatiently waiting for answers. Sofia was getting overloaded, and she was grumpy. But she didn't want to feel grumpy. It didn't chime with the person she wanted to be. In other words, she wasn't being authentic.

In our first coaching session, I asked her to tell me the three or four values she wanted to express through her work.

'Professionalism, service and pride,' she replied.

'How would you rate yourself on each of these values now?' I asked her.

'For service, I would give myself a ten out of ten, but for pride I'm scoring pretty low right now. I feel like I can't keep up and it feels terrible. If I'm honest, I'm not a ten on service either, because I'm often brittle and irritated.'

'What's preventing you from reaching ten out of ten on all three values?'

'I'm trying to please everyone and end up running after myself.'

'Is that something you only do here, or is it something you recognise in other areas of your life?'

'Oh no, this is something I have been doing for years,' she laughed.

'Have you paid prices for it?'

'Oh yes!'

We talked about what this habit had done to her marriage and to her reputation in her previous job, and about her chronic tiredness. It became clear to her that she was being led astray by an expectation she had of herself that was making things worse. She wanted people to see her as helpful and supportive, even if that meant giving up lunch breaks and taking work home at night.

'What's the benefit?'

'There is no benefit,' she said.

'Yes, there is. Otherwise, you would have stopped this years ago.'

She paused for a second.

'Well, I like to think of myself as a helpful person. I suppose I'm afraid of disappointing people,' she admitted.

'And how does this manifest in how you behave and react?'

'I rarely say no. I try to be as flexible as possible. I put other people's needs before my own.'

'And what problems does that create for you?'

'I feel chronically tired and grumpy.'

'So, what do you need to do differently?'

It was clear that this question took Sofia to an uncomfortable place. Initially, she resisted answering the question with excuses – that the queries were critical, and a mistake could cost the company millions; that she had done everything she could; that there weren't any other options; that she couldn't just let the newbies struggle...

'OK, so what are you going to do?' I asked.

She smiled as she recognised her own resistance and that she was making other things more important than solving the underlying issue. She took a deep breath and told me she was going to start by planning consultation hours when she was available and clearly communicating when those hours were, making sure everyone knew where to find the FAQs page and clarifying expectations with team leaders.

'And if you do those things, how would you then rate yourself on professionalism, service and pride?'

'Then I'd be ten out of ten for all of them.'

Through our conversation, Sofia realised that there were a whole lot of questions that she had not asked herself. She had been aware of her problematic habit and had asked herself why it was happening. She'd answered that question with explanations that seemed reasonable, like, 'This person only joined the company last month,' or, 'It's important that this matter is taken seriously and that they don't forget X.'

However, these explanations didn't help her to stop what she was doing. In fact, they did the opposite, justifying what she was doing. She had been working hard and finding more reasons why she couldn't stop, and so the vicious circle continued.

When I got her to ask a different question – 'What am I going to do?' – she saw that she was making her excuses more important than the solution, and that her desire to be needed was perpetuating the problem. The next week I asked her to update me on her progress according to the five sources of success:

'So, tell me. Actions? Results? Identified mistakes? Insights? New knowledge from this past week?'

She answered smiling. 'I planned a week that worked for me. I made it clear when I was available for questions, and I stuck to my plan, which felt great. I also communicated my "opening hours" to the company, and do you know what? No one objected.' She laughed.

'That sounds like an insight.'

'Yes. The insight is that when I stop thinking for others, it is much easier than I thought to solve a problem.'

'Is that an insight you can use elsewhere?'

'Absolutely. I'm going to apply this one with my partner too.'

She went on to explain that since creating clear 'consultation hours' she had noticed that her internal clients had more patience and that the consultations she gave were less stressed, more thorough and far more professional.

'I now feel proud of the work I do, and I have time for jokes and the occasional bit of craziness with my colleagues, which makes life much more fun.'

Your ninth assignment: Choosing and living your values

It takes strong drive to get beyond the pull of your comfort zone and get past your fear of what others may think of you. It should be a drive that you can sustain. When you are driven to create something that you believe in and that makes sense to you, you will discover a strength and resilience you didn't know you had. You will find ways of dealing with setbacks and will be determined to solve any problems you face on the way.

You will find that for something you genuinely care about, you will be willing to invest time and effort to make it happen, and that you even enjoy it. If you have a problem with your Wi-Fi, you get it repaired; if your client misunderstands your email, you get on the phone to fix it. When you are driven by a deep belief in something, obstacles that would otherwise hold you back for a month get resolved in seconds.

You want your goals to reflect what you believe in and consider important. They are an expression of what you value the most. When we dig below the surface of our everyday lives, all of us have our own sense of what is important and what we want to nourish and encourage in life. Whether we have thought about it or not, we find some values more important than others. For some people, generosity is at the top of their list. For others, it's sustainability; for others, it could be empowerment, security or adventure.

The benefit of thinking about what values are important to you is that you make a conscious choice. Much of life just happens, and we fall into habits and routines without noticing. We default to our logical thinking and, before we know it, we react to life in ways that don't reflect how we want to be.

Choosing your values is about making a commitment to handle the present in a way that works for you and makes you proud. Choosing three or four values to guide your day will give you something to hold onto and you can use them to correct any bad habits in your comfort zone: if you tend to get impatient and disconnect from whoever you're with or whatever you're doing, the values of listening, caring or being present could support you to change that habit. If you tend to be chaotic and have a hundred different plans on the go, the values of focus or planning will help. If you tend to keep your thoughts and questions to yourself, valuing honesty or courage will challenge you to speak up. If you have a habit of talking a lot and 'telling it how it is', openness to other perspectives will support you to become a better listener. If you tend to work yourself into the ground, then the value 'pride' will challenge you to stop and reflect on the successes passing you by unnoticed on a daily basis, and so on.

ASSIGNMENT NINE

Your ninth assignment is to identify the value that would most improve your quality of life and give three examples of how it would look in practice. What would you do differently? Then choose to live that value. Carry those actions out and take notes on how it goes and what insights you gain.

TEN

Replace Self-criticism
With Self-Respect

There is an implicit story in our culture that education stops when you graduate or reach adulthood. From then on, it is assumed that you are a finished product and sufficiently developed, so if your manager offers you coaching it means something is wrong.

A lot of people make the process of personal development a painful one because, rather than feeling proud of their progress, they turn every new lesson into a source of self-criticism. It's a sneaky piece of self-manipulation. When they identify something they weren't previously aware of and that they can improve, they see it as proof that they weren't good enough, rather than proof that they dared to grow! They think, 'Why did I do that?' Without realising it, they are beating themselves up for the progress they have made. Logical thinking at its worst. If criticising yourself becomes a regular pattern of thinking, you will quickly find that you don't like or respect yourself much.

What most people have forgotten is that life is an iterative process. In the Middle Ages, if you got ill doctors would let leeches suck your blood because they thought that would make you better. Early in its history, tobacco was seen as a 'cure all' remedy for dressing wounds and reducing pain. Until the 1950s, advertising campaigns made health claims to promote brands of cigarettes.[27] It wasn't until the 1940s that 'epidemiological studies showed a clear link between smoking and lung cancer'.[28] Every day we discover something we were wrong about yesterday. That is progress.

Life is an endless series of discoveries that what we believed in good faith yesterday, was wrong. The problem is, we don't like to *admit* we were wrong. We see it as a sign of ignorance and failure. We hate our mistakes and try our best to hide them and, if that is not

---

27 TL Swedrock, A Hyland and JL Hastrup, 'Changes in the focus of cigarette advertisements in the 1950s' (letter to the editor), *Tobacco Control*, 8 (1999), pp111–112

28 M Tontonoz, 'How do cigarettes cause cancer?', Memorial Sloan Kettering Cancer Center (2018), www.mskcc.org/news/how-do -cigarettes-cause-cancer, accessed September 2021

possible, we make a big show of criticising ourselves for making them.

There is a counterintuitive benefit to self-criticism, because the hidden statement when we criticise ourselves is, 'I know better.' It's a sophisticated trick of our ego-driven logic, where we try to out-think ourselves. But incessant self-criticism comes at the price of our happiness. Every time you criticise yourself – and a lot of us can be very aggressive in doing this – you undermine your respect and love for the human being you are. You are not a robot or an algorithm; you are human. Your humanity is responsible for your commitment to moral codes, your sensitivity and your ability to reflect, to imagine and think things into existence. Take care of and nourish that humanity. Don't fall into the trap of forgetting that, of working like a mule and burning out. These three principles can help you to replace self-criticism with self-respect:

1. **Let the past and the future be.** Focus on what you can influence now. When you pin all your hopes on achieving a goal in the future, you never know whether you will get there. You cannot control the future. Meanwhile, the past has been and gone – you have no control over that, either. You are living with the legacy of the past, but you can't change it. If you fight against what has already happened, you will never win and will waste your present. You can choose how to deal with your present.

2. **Choose values that make you proud**, that you genuinely find important. Don't make the mistake of aligning yourself with the values you think you *ought* to choose, or that others want you to choose. You cannot fool yourself. The values you should choose are those that will make you proud of the person you are. As these values manifest in the way you relate to your loved ones and the people in your life, it will bring you a deep sense of fulfilment.

3. **Change your metric for intelligence**. Your university degree, scholarships and accolades may have landed you a job with a nice salary in a cool company. It's not surprising if you feel the need to show you are smart enough to handle the projects you are given, to measure up against your co-workers. But if you find yourself hating the fact that you made a mistake, or trying to show that you know better, you might want to think again. For most people, the truth is you will rarely be the person in the room who knows the most; there will always be someone who knows more than you. What's more, your craft is developing at an ever-increasing speed. There is always more to learn and more to know. Living in the story of separation and competition, you may see this as a threat, but in the story of connectedness this room to grow is space to express yourself and show your true colours.

Case study: Sara

Sara was a developer and had been doing a good job guiding a project team through a phase of significant changes. One day, her manager invited her into his office and told her about an upcoming vacancy that she might want to consider applying for. It was a product manager position, which would mean a considerable step up in seniority and salary. His opinion was that if she built her confidence in a few areas, she would stand a good chance of getting it. He gave her a tip: 'Learn to show up even when things are uncertain and changing and you will be a strong candidate for that position.'

She got in touch with me, and we had our first meeting. I asked her what her reasons were for pursuing the coaching and what she wanted to get out of it. She told me she wanted to increase her self-esteem and we agreed that the values of clarity and self-confidence could support her.

She explained that the new position was in another team and was currently held by an interim manager. The team had only recently been formed and she knew very little about what they were working on. Meanwhile, she had her hands full in her own team and would have to reallocate tasks and see that things were going smoothly before she could free herself up.

I asked her to make a simple plan, which she did. It was as follows:

- **Week 1–2:**

  – Prepare her current project group to continue without her, by supporting them to identify their challenges and make plans to handle them

  – Get to know the interim manager of the new team and pick his brains about the team and their challenges

- **Week 3–4:**

  – Shadow the interim manager

  – Sit in on meetings of the new team and learn what's going on

Next, I asked her to make a list of actions. She filled a page with a list that included a series of phone calls and emails to arrange meetings and cups of coffee with the interim manager and several people in her project team. That week, her homework was to carry out these actions.

The next week, we started the meeting by looking at success in general.

'Tell me, what needs to happen for you to think you are doing well?' I asked her.

'I'm not sure,' she replied. 'I guess when I see that my efforts are paying off.'

'And what moments are those?'

'When I get a compliment from my manager, when we complete a project on time, when a client is happy. Things like that.'

'OK, fine. I'm going to create a category for those moments and call it "achieved wanted results". Agreed?'

'Yes.'

'For most people, the indicator of success is achieving results they want to achieve. Now I'm going to give you four more categories. The second category is actions you took that you wanted to take. Any actions. It could be phoning a co-worker to check something, researching a holiday or asking your babysitter to work this weekend. Any action, regardless of the results.'

Sara looked doubtful.

'Why is an action a source of success?' I asked her.

'I'm not sure,' she reflected.

'Because you could have postponed your phone call to your co-worker for another month, but you didn't. Instead of contacting your babysitter to ask about this weekend, you could have given up before you started and assumed going out with your husband was out of the question.'

'OK, yes. I see.'

'Why is an action a source of success regardless of the result?'

'Because if I don't take an action, the results will never happen,' she said, tentatively.

'That's part of it. Without the action, there is no result. You can't know before you take the action what the result will be, so the action is in itself a success. If the action doesn't create a wanted reaction, can you learn from it?'

'Yes.'

'So whatever the result, the action has created progress for you.'

I then took her through all five sources of success:

1. An achieved, wanted result – including any bonus results you hadn't expected.

2. Action taken.

3. New knowledge, anything you learned – you learned some words of Dutch; you found out about a new computer programme function; you figured out how to use Zoom on your phone. Any new knowledge is a source of success because it makes you more effective.

4. Insight. Whenever you think, 'Aha! I've never looked at it this way before,' you've had an insight. An insight is not the same as new knowledge. While new knowledge is about new information, an insight is a new perspective.

5. An identified mistake.

Talking about the last of these points, I explained to Sara, 'The mistake itself is not the success, the success is in identifying the mistake. For example, if I don't realise that my way of talking to my colleague irritates them, can I correct that behaviour?'

'No.'

'So I might make that mistake hundreds of times without realising it. The success is in the moment I realise that my way is not working, which will allow me to correct myself in the future. Clear?'

'I think so.'

I then gave Sara a few minutes to write down her sources of success from the past week, using this list, and asked her to talk me through them.

'I had quite a good morning with the interim manager,' she said.

'What made it good?'

'He talked me through a lot of what has been going on.'

'It sounds like you learned a lot of important information, is that true?'

'Yes.'

'It also sounds like the atmosphere between you was open and honest. Am I right?'

'Yes.'

'How did you achieve that? What was it in the way you approached the conversation that created that atmosphere? Did you explain the context of why you wanted to sit with him?'

'Yes, I did.'

'Did you take his style of communication into account?'

'Yes. I saw that he was an informal type, so I was chatty and interested and went with the flow rather than trying to be structured and get straight to the point.'

After a few minutes of discussion, Sara recognised that this one conversation had included the following points, every one of which was a success:

- Results:

  – Constructive conversation

  – Congenial atmosphere

  – Deeper trust

- Actions:

  – Initiated the conversation

  – Considered his style of communication

  – Went with the flow

  – Was chatty and funny

  – Listened

- New knowledge:

  – Who the team members are

  – What their roles are

  – What the targets are

  – What the main challenges and difficulties are

  – What has been tried

Reviewing this list, Sara had an insight: she had never looked this way at her work. She took it as a given that things generally went smoothly, and she had never given herself credit for it. By dissecting her progress, she saw how many little steps she had taken along the way.

'Do you realise that, if you had approached the conversation with him in a formal and technical way, you would probably have created resistance?'

'I suppose so. I never looked at it that way before.'

'Do you see, then, that it is not a coincidence that the conversation went so well?'

'I do now.'

'The atmosphere in the conversation would have been strained and you wouldn't have learned as much about the team and the challenges they are facing,' I explained.

In response, she added two more successes to her list:

- Insight: That it was not a coincidence that the conversation went smoothly

- Identified mistake: Not giving myself credit when conversations go well

'OK, great. Let's leave the successes for now,' I said. 'How did your week go? Did you take all the actions you planned?'

'Yes, I was really in action. I sat in on a meeting with the interim manager and got a good sense of what was going on in the team. I also had a conversation with him that went well. He took time to talk me through a lot of what was going on, which helped. Meanwhile, my current team completed our route map for the coming year and I presented it to my managers. I guess that went OK.'

'What do you mean it went OK?' I asked.

'Well, they approved it, but it didn't feel like the meeting went well.'

'Why not?'

'They just sat there listening. They asked a few tricky questions, which I answered, and then they approved it.'

'Which is what you wanted, right?'

'Yes, but they were so distant, hard and impersonal. As they always are. There is never a smile or a compliment, a "You did great!" Without that, I start to doubt whether I am doing OK. It's always like this with my boss. He never has time. Meetings are always extremely short and business-like. Sometimes I just need to hear that I'm doing well.'

'And what if that doesn't happen?'

'I wonder what I'm doing wrong, and I start looking for my mistakes. I become super-critical of myself, and my conclusion is always that I'm not doing well enough.'

'Do you think that's what he believes?'

'No, I know he is pleased with me and thinks I'm doing well. Otherwise, he wouldn't be encouraging me to go for this job. It's just he is so economical with compliments, but I need them.'

'Have you ever told him that you would like to receive praise from time to time?' She shook her head. 'So maybe it's time you do. If the way he supports you doesn't work for you, doesn't that class as a mistake on his part?'

'Yes, I suppose so.'

'If it's something that's important for you, why don't you tell him?'

'I am going to.'

'How often do you give yourself compliments?'

'Not often.'

'Why not?'

'I am just so used to checking where I might have missed something, where I need to correct. I guess I am pretty hard on myself.'

We had a conversation about this, and I set her a homework task of sending me an email everyday with at least ten successes, which she did. Every day, she noted details of how she had ensured things had gone smoothly at home by planning well, arranging babysitters and not fighting moments when things didn't go to plan; how she dared to address sensitive subjects in conversation with the interim manager; how she had noticed he was grumpy and seen it as his problem rather than hers. The following week, she was relaxed and proud of the progress she was making. She told me that the interim manager had suggested a transition period in which he supported her to ease into the new role. She should take the lead in the team and he would take a step back and be there for support.

Your tenth assignment: Harvesting mistakes

You may have learned that knowing stuff and being a brilliant thinker will get you to where you want to be. You need to forget that. If you want to thrive and be happy in tech, you need to drop your fear of looking stupid and learn to harvest your mistakes, because that's where the magic is.

I'm not saying that sloppiness is good. The expertise, knowledge and methodologies that you and your team have developed need to be applied with the respect, care and professionalism they warrant. Instead, I'm talking about how you handle uncertainty. You never know before you take an action what the result will

THE GEEK'S GUIDE TO WORK

be. You and your team will frequently face situations in which you have to try out new approaches – in the way you build products, or the way you manage relationships with clients within and outside the company. When dealing with uncertainty, one thing is certain: the wanted result is never guaranteed. There will be times when things don't work out. Most people describe these moments as mistakes and criticise themselves for them. That is flawed thinking that undermines confidence and fritters away unique opportunities for learning.

Harvesting your mistakes means that, if something doesn't work out, instead of chastising yourself, you identify the learning opportunity, embrace it and examine it in detail. Any step in a project is a sequence of hundreds of actions. If something didn't work and you don't identify what that was, you cannot correct it. What's more, you may miss the fact that lots of other actions worked well.

While your ticket into your job may have been IQ, you get things done through teamwork. Your ability to create supportive relationships with others and, above all, with yourself is critical. You are part of an ecosystem of people and together your task is to translate a complex, ambitious and sometimes nebulous briefing into a sophisticated set of interconnected parts. In doing so, there will be issues to handle with both clients and colleagues. In other words, there are lots of moving parts in the tech world. Your job is about creating the social lubrication to allow these parts to move with as little tension and as much learning, partnership and inspiration as possible.

ASSIGNMENT TEN

Your tenth assignment is to write down at least five examples for each of these points:

- Actions that you wanted to take, and you took. This can be any action of any kind. If you took it, it counts.

- New knowledge or information you learned, about any subject.

- Wanted results that you achieved. This can be any result you wanted to create, whether measurable or an intangible atmosphere, write it down.

- Mistakes you are now aware of. Getting to the bottom of what it was you didn't know or do, or the way you did something, will help you in the future. Harvest this information to support yourself to grow.

- Any insights, epiphanies or realisations you had that may be useful in the future.

Summary: Authenticity

- Being authentic is about outsmarting your logical thinking, ego and fear, and learning to be the person you can and want to be. Self-awareness is the process of getting to and maintaining your authenticity.

- If we don't have a plan, life chooses for us, and we end up spending our time in ways we later regret. The idea that planning is about girding and disciplining yourself into action is rooted in the story of separation. The hidden message is that without it, you aren't good enough. In the story of connectedness, we don't need girding because we have a surfeit of energy and motivation. In this context, planning is about choosing and pursuing a direction for yourself.

- Every choice we make has consequences. Choosing one direction rules out another. Many people avoid making choices because they don't want to live with the consequences. They cannot win, because without paying the price you can't reap the benefits. A wholehearted choice involves knowing and accepting that choosing one option rules out others.

- A lot of people base their choices on what they think they *should* choose, or what others have chosen, rather than what is most important for them. This can happen without us realising it. Our mind thinks for us. When you consciously choose a direction for yourself, one that you genuinely care about, you will find a resilience you didn't know you had.

- Life is an iterative process. Learning to be OK with admitting that what you thought yesterday was wrong, is key to improving your results and increasing your happiness. A lot of people make the process of personal development a painful one because they turn their lessons into a source of self-criticism rather than of pride.

ELEVEN

Four People Who Wanted To Make A Difference – But Nearly Didn't

This is a cautionary tale of four people who never met each other: Bill, Lakshmi, Tatjana and Mo.

Bill, in his late fifties, was a manager for a Dutch scale-up running an important worldwide environmental project. He had spent much of his career in management teams and non-executive boards and looked forward to using his experience to make a difference in the world. When I met him half an hour before the programme, all that was worrying him was his habit of destroying relationships, including his marriage.

Just four days into the programme, Bill shared with the group that he had been in senior positions in various large NGOs where there had been so much internal politics that he had become disillusioned. When I asked him how he dealt with it, he was honest enough to confess that his way of coping had been to mentally disengage. 'There was not much I could do, and honestly, I didn't want the confrontation. I had my hands full dealing with my own life.'

When I asked him how someone in his position could be so cynical, he looked shocked. He thought I was joking. Sometime after the training, he thanked me for the wakeup call and said that he realised he'd been sticking his head in the sand. Having reconsidered his options, he had decided to initiate conversations with senior colleagues to put the subject of the organisation's culture on the agenda.

Lakshmi was a PhD student in environmental science, a young woman who believed passionately that society needed to make huge changes to prevent climate disaster. She was vegan, bought only second-hand clothes, monitored her carbon footprint closely and was highly committed to doing whatever she could to be part of the change that needed to happen. There was only one problem: she was chronically angry. She had come to the training because of fights with her boyfriend and, within an hour, she had got into a disagreement with one of the assistants in the team. In almost every conversation, she expressed her disbelief about why things were the way they were. She frequently asked questions like, 'How come X? Why Z?' Her exasperation had become an integral part of how she presented herself. She was adamant about how things 'should' be and, for the other trainees and the team, she was an uncomfortable presence to be around.

At one point in the training, the penny dropped: she realised that on her own she was never going to make a significant difference to climate change, and that until now her attitude had made her an island. People avoided her. If she was truly committed to her values, she was going to have to join forces with as many people and organisations as possible. She needed to overcome the anger and become someone other people enjoyed being around and learning from.

Mo had just finished university and was working for a company offering outdoor training. He was a sensitive young man, interested in the world around him. He was aware of problems in the way a lot of things in society were run – the education system, the way the elderly were treated, the financial system, the housing market and the hours people spent working in jobs they didn't like. Meanwhile, he was trying to figure out what he wanted to do in life and hoped the training would help him learn to speak up more and stand his ground.

During the training, Mo participated in a game in which the objective was to win points. The previous day he had noticed his tendency to sit back and let others lead, so in this task he decided to take the lead. When he stood up, there were several discussions going on in the group at the same time, but he dared to speak up and cut through the noise. He brought his group together, getting everyone to listen to each other so that the group made progress and achieved results.

There was one small problem, which was that Mo forgot to stop and ask himself what his own definition of success was. What was the point of all this? Like a technocrat, he was so focused on getting the team working and winning points that he ended up leading them towards a result he wasn't proud of.

Tatjana was a marketing executive working for a multinational. With her intellect and straightforward leadership style, she had proven her ability to create results in teams. The career ladder had taken her from her home country of Ukraine, via Russia and England, to the company headquarters in the Netherlands. She had things sorted: a good position with a good salary, good prospects, a nice boyfriend and a nice apartment. In her spare time, she liked to read and attend lectures about social and economic innovations to help improve society.

She had signed up for the programme because she wasn't getting any satisfaction out of her job. Although she was paid well, respected and had a good role in the company, she missed having a sense of meaning. One week after the training, she told me she had quit her job and gone to join her boyfriend who lived in Geneva, where she was going to do a master's degree in European and International governance. Now she works for the UN, developing smart and sustainable cities.

These are four people who wanted to change the world for the better, but almost did the exact opposite without realising it. Bill was in a position of influence but was caught up in his self-created personal problems. Tatjana had the talent and competencies, but her golden cage was just too comfortable. Lakshmi was a visionary who was too angry to inspire anyone or lead a change. Mo was so anxious to be part of the action that he turned into a technocrat with no moral compass.

The moral of this story is that saying you want change and making it happen are two entirely different things.

Conclusion

Being a human on this planet is a huge privilege. We have had the opportunity to develop and expand our influence to such an extent that 8.7 million species of plants and animals are now dependent on our choices. Whatever we may think about the rights and wrongs of this and how this happened, what brought us to this place is an extraordinary combination of qualities present in every human. From the ability to read our environment, move in it and shape it; to the ability to intuit, be creative, to communicate ideas, even to large numbers of strangers; to the ability to develop moral codes, experience emotion, be moved and create deep relationships even in surroundings that are challenging and violent.

In our culture, we are frequently told that certain geniuses have more brilliant qualities than others. This is a lie. It's also quite convenient, because it lets the rest of us off the hook and allows us to settle with whatever average level of happiness, success and influence we have. One of the side effects is that we look to these 'geniuses' as role models and many extraordinary human qualities have not had their value recognised.

The only thing that is different about people who are happier or brilliant at what they do is that they have gone to work with themselves and put in the hours to get there. They have developed the self-discipline to beat their demons time and again. The reason I have devoted my life to this work is that I believe that when more individuals from more backgrounds do the work, show their true colours and become happier, more effective and more influential, our collective future will be brighter.

I hope this book has shown you that while personal development is not always easy, you can learn to turn any situation that is not working for you into a breakthrough that immediately benefits you, your co-workers and your loved ones. When you adopt this approach, life becomes an incredibly exciting journey towards greater wisdom. In the coming months, use the HACCA model to focus yourself, develop your alertness to situations in your working and private life, and increase your effectiveness and determination to handle them.

Next Steps

Go to https://juliasullivan.scoreapp.com and take the Inspiring Leader Questionnaire to find out where your strengths and weaknesses lie. You will find out what you can focus on to become more inspiring for yourself and the people you work and live with. It may also explain why you are struggling in certain areas.

If you are interested in doing some personal development work and this approach appeals to you, why don't you join me on a Soft Skills For Excellence Programme? It's a three-day online programme during which you will create alignment and trust where they are needed, both at work and at home. As a reader of this book, you are entitled to a 30% discount on the programme. Just go to Juliasullivan.nl/book-my-spot and use the code HACCAgeek to claim your discount.

I also offer a one-hour live consultation for leaders in organisations. If you want to discuss the challenges you're facing and how a tailormade programme for you and your team could help, go to Juliasullivan.nl /free-consult to make an appointment.

Acknowledgements

The process of writing this book was a journey of ups and downs throughout which I have been inspired and supported by so many people. Lucy McCarraher and Joe Gregory, who lead the Rethink Bookbuilder programme, first relit my writing spark back in December 2020, and both have been true rocks. Thanks also to my editors, Kathleen Steeden and Abigail Angus, who have done a great job of tightening everything up.

I owe thanks to my beta readers, who were valiant enough to read the first version (which in no way resembled the final book), and for the kind and encouraging way they told me I might need to throw away the first version and go back to the drawing board. Thank you to Jens Langendorff, who suggested back in January 2020 that I write a second book. (Thanks Jens for replying to the messages I sent during my thinking

THE GEEK'S GUIDE TO WORK

trips on the racing bike.) To Paul Heijmans, for sending your clear and useful response bang on time and on brief. Anneke Holl, for the conversations we had about the human side of startups, and for the input you gave during a busy and challenging time. Joep Piscaer, thank you for the great conversation we had in your kitchen when you confirmed how critical personal development is in tech. Miguel Ferreira, for the straight and thoughtful way you say what you think, and for your swift responses to my queries. Lieke Hallegraaf, for giving me an under-thirty-five's perspective on life in tech. James Montgomery, for immediately saying yes to my question of whether you would consider reading the manuscript. Janneke Maas, for your friendship and support, both as a beta reader and in the training room. Finally, thank you, Stefan Timmerman, for offering to beta-read the book without even knowing me.

I am indebted to Linda Bovaird for hiring me in 2014 to support her team and thereby introducing me into the tech world, for the many opportunities we have had to work and chat together since then, and for being a true ambassador for personal development in this industry. Thanks also to her husband, Sean, for sharing his memories as a young tech people manager, and for hooking me up with others who he thought could help.

Thanks to Jouk Pleiter for originally suggesting Linda and I talk in 2014, and for investing in the personal development of 100 of his company's top leaders, thereby starting my career off in this new direction.

I would like to thank my friends for hearing me out when I was struggling with a chapter, and my dear Humanication partners Yiftach, Lilyan, Cesar, Carrol, Cathelijne, Suzanne, Onn, Ayelet, Ezri, Saar, Nizan and Liran, who continue to inspire me with their wisdom, courage and determination to create a society led by humanity rather than fear.

Last, but not by any means least, thank you to my beloved husband, Robbert, who knows what it is to write, who listened patiently when I got overexcited or had a bad day; and who challenged, inspired and coached me to carry on.

The Author

Julia Sullivan has spent the past twenty years supporting individuals, teams and organisations to create inspiring, collaborative and sustainable working environments that can contribute to a healthy future. The wealth of unused intelligence, creativity and sensitivity that she encounters daily gives her hope. Together with a team of world-class personal development facilitators, she has supported organisations within and outside of Europe to improve their results, reduce sick leave and truly engage great talent by tapping into this hidden human potential. Most of this work is done via live programmes, which a participant once described as 'exhilarating multiple-day experiences'.

Julia came to this work in 1996 when, as a young marketeer working for Levi Strauss & Co, she came close to burnout, and went looking for answers to questions like, what is intelligence? What is leadership? What is happiness?

Julia's introduction to tech came by chance in 2014 when a professional services manager asked her to run some programmes for an international team. She was then asked back to co-design and run a leadership journey for 100 of the company's top leaders worldwide. Since then, she has run workshops, training programmes and executive coaching programmes for some of Europe's leading fintech and retail tech companies, many of which are in the Netherlands.

Julia was born and educated in England, has two grown-up sons, and lives with her Dutch husband, Robbert, in Amsterdam.

🌐 www.Juliasullivan.nl

in www.linkedin.com/in/jusullivan

📷 @JuliaKSullivan

Printed in Great Britain
by Amazon